W9-CNB-600

Standing the Test of Time

STANDING THE TEST OF TIME

LOVE STORIES OF AFRICAN AMERICAN ELDERS

Julie Rainbow

THE PILGRIM PRESS
CLEVELAND

The Pilgrim Press, 700 Prospect Avenue, Cleveland, Ohio 44115-1100
pilgrimpress.com

© 2001 by Julie Rainbow

All rights reserved. Published 2001

Printed in the United States of America on acid-free paper

06   05   04   03   02   01   5   4   3   2   1

Library of Congress Cataloging-in-Publication Data

Standing the test of time : love stories of African American elders / [compiled by] Julie Rainbow.
     p.   cm.
   ISBN 0-8298-1434-5 (alk. paper)
    1. African American families—Biography—Anecdotes.   2. Married people—United States—
Biography—Anecdotes.   3. African American families—Social conditions—Anecdotes.
4. Married people—United States—Social conditions—Anecdotes.   5. Love—United States—
Anecdotes.   6. Marriage—United States—Anecdotes.   7. Devotion—Anecdotes.
8. Man-woman relationships—United States—Anecdotes.   I. Rainbow, Julie, 1960–

E185.86.S6977   2001
920'.009296073—dc21
                                                              2001044606

DEDICATED TO RENA ENNIS,

WHO MADE HER TRANSITION JUNE 18, 1995.

Rena and her husband Rudy Ennis were the
first couple interviewed for this project.

CONTENTS

PREFACE xi

1 LOOKING FOR PEACE AND TRUTH — Hattie and Ralph Wilson 1

2 OUR HISTORY WAS PARALLEL — Dorothy and Holman Edmond 9

3 BECOMING WHOLE — Eva and Van Bird 18

4 THE BEST OF FRIENDS — Jean and Lester Sloan 26

5 STRAIGHT UP AND FOR REAL — Bettye and Willie Bozeman 34

6 BELIEVING IN A BEING GREATER THAN OURSELVES — Irene and Joseph Yarbrough 43

7 BUILDING A MARRIAGE — Auretha and Jethro English 52

8 GOOD AND TRUE FRIENDS — Rena and Rudy Ennis 61

9 EVOLVING TOGETHER — Sylvia and Robert Bozeman 69

10 WE ARE IN THIS UNTIL THE END — Brenda and Aaron Turpeau 76

11 RESPECT EACH OTHER AS INDIVIDUALS — Patricia and Geoffrey Heard 85

12 BLIND DATE — Pauline and Charles Coffey 95

13 THROUGH THICK AND THIN — Mary and Rupert Ferebee 103

14 GIVE AND TAKE — Bernese and Archie Meyer 110

15 WEATHERING THE STORMS — Jeri and Adell Mills 116

16 READY FOR COMMITMENT — Louise and George Shipman 125

17 SUNSHINE AND SHADOWS — E. Vivian and Louis Williams 132

18 MAY YOUR WAY BE SMOOTHED AND BRIGHTENED — Dorothy and Paul McGirt 140

19 UNDERSTANDING THE POSSIBILITIES — Vera and Thad Taylor 146

20 ACTIONS SPEAK LOUDER THAN WORDS — Dorothy and Cleveland Lassiter 152

THE LOVE WHICH HAS LASTED

IS THE LOVE WHICH HAS

EVERYTHING

EVERY DISAPPOINTMENT, EVERY

FAILURE,

WHICH HAS ACCEPTED THE FACT THAT

IN THE END THERE IS NO DESIRE

SO DEEP

AS THE SIMPLE DESIRE FOR

BEING WITH EACH OTHER.

—Graham Greene

PREFACE

After my first marriage ended in divorce, the hurt and anger were gripping. As I moved beyond the hurt and anger, the feeling of confusion continued. Though my marriage had been difficult at times, I believed that we would get through the rough times if we put forth the effort to work out our issues—in other words, stay together, by any means necessary. However, my husband at the time felt differently. He left our marriage without giving me a clue as to the "real" reason for his departure.

With this confusion, I sought solace from those individuals who had always given me comfort during difficult periods in my life—our elders. While I was in the midst of the healing process, elders imparted words of wisdom, provided shoulders to cry on, and shared alternate perspectives of marriage, which were different from the narrow scopes of romantic love that I had been embracing. Their stories were rich with understanding and hope. Through these shared discussions, the pain and confusion soon dissipated and were replaced with a renewed sense of understanding and hope.

Upon sharing the insights I gained from the elders with my friends and family, I was encouraged to continue systematically the work I was doing. Soon thereafter, a research project had begun. This was the beginning of *Standing the Test of Time*. This book documents the trials and tribulations of African American couples who have been married more than thirty years. They have survived the social upheavals, economic turbulence, and personal disappointments that often tear families apart. While I was in their presence, these couples radiated a connectedness and deep bond of acceptance and love for one another.

The stories shared in *Standing the Test of Time* are filled with humor, joy, sadness, and pain. While teaching us that love is a paradox not meant for the faint-hearted to pursue, they also show that being married can take us to the heights of ecstasy, in which everything is possible. Love can also pillage us to the depths of despair, from which we must reach for the light within our souls in order to forgive.

With much gratitude, appreciation and love, I would like to thank all the couples who were interviewed for this book. They allowed me to enter their private lives as they shared stories about their marriages. Though I was not able to use the stories of all the couples I met over the duration of this project, I am grateful for everyone's willingness to share.

Alex Jones, the photographer, shared my vision of this project and was willing to use his photographic expertise to take the updated portraits of each couple that open the chapters. (Julie Yarbrough photographed her parents, Irene and Joseph Yarbrough.) I am grateful for his commitment thoughout the process.

My family and friends were the foundation that kept me going during periods of doubt and exhaustion. Seymour Douglas, my partner in marriage, has challenged me in unbelievable ways to grow and heal, even without his knowing, and for this I am hopeful that we, too, may have many years together.

This book is to be used as a guide to create healthy, loving relationships. In reading about these ordinary people who made their commitment to one another a priority, we become aware that this is a possibility we all may experience. The couples in *Standing the Test of Time* exemplify the resolve needed to experience "real love." Though married thirty years or more, they continue to enjoy being married to their beloved. Sit down, be still, and let the love these couples radiate encircle your heart.

STANDING THE TEST OF TIME

1

LOOKING FOR PEACE AND TRUTH

HATTIE AND RALPH WILSON

Married May 7, 1949 · Elkton, Maryland

Hattie! Hattie, the telephone!" Hattie recalls hearing. "I knew it was Ralph because he was the only person that ever called me at college. You were 'hot stuff' if somebody called you, and when he called, he was always somewhere different. Because he traveled a lot, I began to fantasize that this rich boy was going to get me out of this small town. He traveled and that was appealing to me."

"In the beginning I didn't have any particular affection for Hattie," Ralph admits. "I did for her, the same as I had done for my sisters. It was my pattern. I had sent my two sisters to school before I met Hattie. She was in school trying to 'make it,' so if I could help her with the money I was making, I would. It wasn't a strain."

"At first, I didn't like him. He had just gotten out of the service, and one day a friend and I were walking down Duke Street in Lancaster, Pennsylvania. This fella comes up and offers to buy us a drink. I was horrified that somebody would offer to buy me a drink or even think that I would drink alcohol. That was really horrifying to me, so I didn't like him because of that. At the time I was nineteen. To me, he didn't respect me. He talked all the time and always had a camera around his neck. The second time I remember seeing him was at church. He threw his hat in my lap, which was

HATTIE, AT AGE 18, ONE MONTH
AFTER HIGH SCHOOL GRADUATION IN 1944,
LANCASTER, PENNSYLVANIA.

RALPH WILSON, WHILE IN THE
UNITED STATES AIRFORCE, 1940S.

a sign that he wanted me to be his girl. I didn't want to be branded as anybody's girl. He wasn't my boyfriend," states Hattie adamantly.

"I threw the hat in her lap because I didn't want to put it on the seat," Ralph laughs.

"Soon after the church incident, he started calling me at college, Cheyney," Hattie continues. "I really didn't pay him that much attention, even though he was calling."

"After a while he grew on me and I knew he liked me. He had excellent manners, was always attentive, opened doors for me, and all that 'good stuff,' which I wasn't accustomed to. I read about it in books, but the people were always white. I used to read a lot and back then blacks couldn't go to the public library, so whenever I would get a dime I would buy these 'Street & Smith' love stories."

"As for manners, I was raised in a house full of women. My mother didn't know, but since my mother knew she didn't know, she copied the people where she worked. She would copy what she saw and heard on the job," Ralph explains. "By this time, I knew I liked Hattie, and we began to communicate more."

"I liked Ralph, too, but I didn't know whether I really wanted to get married. Finishing school was my goal. However, he continued to pursue and bought me a platinum set of rings. I asked him to take those rings back, because I had to finish school. As a senior I needed the extra money to graduate and the rings were expensive. He took them back and bought another ring. He didn't buy a set, he bought me one ring. After we had gotten the license, I decided I didn't want to get married, so I gave him back the ring. He rolled up the receipt for the license, put the ring around it and threw it away."

"She didn't want, I didn't want it," Ralph insists.

"After giving it some thought, I decided I liked him enough to marry him. One Saturday morning I left campus, met Ralph in Westchester, and we went to Maryland to get married, in Elkton, Maryland. We got married in Maryland, because we didn't need a blood test. We went to the minister's house, paid ten dollars, and got married. There were three or four couples ahead of us. When the minister was marrying them, he would look out the window. I said, 'Uh-uh, we're not doing it like this.' When our time came I told him, 'I'm pulling down these shades, so when you marry me I don't want you looking out the window to see how many ten dollars are coming in that door, because I don't intend to do this but once. I want you to give us your full attention.' I told the minister, 'When you say 'let us pray,' wait until we kneel and then pray over us. Don't start praying, no, no, no, we must kneel first.'"

"I wasn't paying attention to him," Ralph offers.

"He took Ralph in the kitchen and told him, 'Don't marry that girl because she's too bossy.'"

"It was too late then," Ralph laughs.

"After we got married, we took the bus to his mother's house. She cooked spaghetti. He was sitting there drinking lemonade and looking at me. I'm eating and he's staring. His mother is upset because he's not eating, so she goes out and buys calf's liver, his favorite, and he didn't eat that either," recalls Hattie.

"I didn't need any food, because when you have a jewel, you enjoy the jewel. I was enjoying the jewel," Ralph says. "I was too busy to eat."

"Shoot, I was eating, because when you're in college, you look forward to some good food, and I was going back to school the next morning," Hattie continues. "I had two more weeks in college and seniors had to be on campus for Sunday school."

"We got married and didn't have a honeymoon," says Ralph.

"Though we didn't have a physical honeymoon there was this point in time where the relationship changed. Being head over heels was over; we had to get down to some serious business and work through this," Hattie explains.

"After marrying, we lived apart for about two weeks," he says.

"Ralph was working in Middletown, Pennsylvania, as an airplane mechanic, so we lived there, but we didn't stay long. We went to live with his mother and sisters. He told me not to do it, but his mother said it was a good move. She was an elder, and you always listened to your elders, that was the way I was raised. I couldn't understand why Ralph didn't want to live with his mother. Later I discovered Ralph was right; it was a bad move. By that time I was pregnant. We stayed there a few weeks and then he disappeared. I hadn't the slightest idea where he was.

"Ralph couldn't take it, it was too much for him, so he ran away to Boston. He was living in a huge house in Boston, where I stayed with him a couple of nights, then we went to Syracuse, where my father lived. Then they called for us to come home because my grandfather was dying. All of this confusion happened during our first year of marriage.

"We were married nine months and eleven days when Paula, our daughter, was born," Hattie continues. "Immediately, I learned that Ralph was different from the men that I was accustomed to. He'd iron but he wouldn't wash. The first month of Paula's birth he washed Paula's clothes because women weren't supposed to put their hands in water. We were pampered. That's the only time he washed. I didn't like ironing. I ironed one shirt for him and he told me not to iron for him anymore."

"Remember, I was raised with a house full of women," Ralph laughs. "It doesn't bother me to be at home. When I'm going to clean, I put her out. My first love and joy is messing in the kitchen. I'm a serious cook and I enjoy it."

"Ralph was different and that was one of the attractions," Hattie says. "I knew he was different from the other fellas when we got married. He takes care of the house. He likes being home, and the first paycheck he got, he gave it to me."

A PROUD RALPH WILSON AND DAUGHTER PAULA AT HER JUNIOR HIGH SCHOOL GRADUATION IN 1965.

"My father always gave his money to my mother. He said, 'As hard as I work, it's easier for her to take care of the money.' My mother always took care of the money, so that's what I was accustomed to; therefore, I did it without even thinking about it," Ralph explains. "My father even went to my mother to get money for cigarettes. It never bothered him."

"When I would get mad I would run away, temporarily," Hattie offers. "I'd leave the house, go stay away all day, come back, and go to bed. When I left I didn't take my worries with me. I'd put my worries on the back burner and as soon as I hit the front door I picked them up again. Ralph would ignore me. I'd ask him a question and he wouldn't answer. That would bug me. If he was displeased with something, he wouldn't talk or say he was displeased with it. How would I know what's going on if he didn't talk? He doesn't do it as much now—he'll answer."

"My mother argued so much and so long, that I disconnected. When I disconnect I cannot answer what I don't hear," Ralph explains. "I could disconnect at the drop of a hat, because my mother would go on for hour after hour after hour. She was a spitfire.

"When I got married I was very confused," Ralph admits. "It took me years to understand what was wrong. I was a boy in a house full of women; consequently, I'm a boy, but I was taught to think like a woman. It was confusion and it took me years to understand what was wrong with me. When a boy is raised with a house full of women, he's confused. I was in total turmoil. It took me years to realize men and women do not think alike.

"I really can't say when I realized there was a problem, but when I did I began to work on it," Ralph offers. "You cannot solve a problem until you see it. That took a long time because it was deeply imbedded. When two people get married they both bring their garbage to the marriage. I realized garbage can do one thing—stink! That's all it can do, and you have to work through that.

"I was raised in confusion," he continues, "therefore, I was looking for one thing—truth."

"I think he had been looking for a long time. He was looking for peace. In looking for peace he found truth," adds Hattie.

"When I found truth, that straightened up the confusion. Christ was the truth. I was looking for Him and didn't realize it until I found Him," says Ralph.

"Of course, I knew there were problems," Hattie recalls, "but they were his problems. At first I thought it was me. We would discuss it, then he would turn it all around and say it was me. We went to see a marriage counselor, and I realized during one of those sessions that he didn't really see me. He was transferring feelings about his mother to me. It wasn't me, it was his mother he was seeing. Initially, it was devastating to realize that I've been married to this man almost thirty years, and he's confused me all these years with his mother. I'm not his mother! We talked about it and worked through that and then there was some light."

"After we worked through that, then he decided that he was an alcoholic. When he told me, I was like, 'so what,' because all the men in my family drank, including my father, but it never kept them from working, nor did it keep Ralph from working. It never kept them from taking care of their family. It didn't mean anything to me."

"I did not drink regularly," Ralph offers.

"Ralph could go for three or four years and not drink. I never thought of him as having a drinking problem. I was accustomed to men drinking, so it was no big deal. My father drank every day and it never kept him from working. I never saw Ralph drunk. When he drank he wanted to dance and play.

"It took me a while to work through that, to understand that. He wanted to go away to rehab. He signed up before he told me. I was ready to hit the ceiling, because how dare you do that and don't discuss it with me."

"I had been running away from something, running away from myself," Ralph admits. "Most people get married for the wrong reason. Men think women are going to complete their lives and solve their problems and women think the same about men. Not so—life comes from inside of you. Something outside of you cannot sustain your life because what you need is on the inside. Learn what is missing on the inside and do the best you can to solve that garbage that you both have before you get married."

"I tried to change him, but he never tried to change me. I've always been able to be my own person. He would encourage me to do things. I can't imagine being married to anybody else. I tell him, nobody wants you but me, and nobody wants me but you. I know I'm not necessarily the easiest person to live with, we just complete each other. A lot of people get married because they're in love. The goal is not to be in love—but to love."

"When we got married," Ralph continues, "I told her if I didn't trust her I wouldn't be marrying her. She's free because I trust her."

"Once he decided we should have separate apartments. He was going to have the key to my apartment, but I wasn't going to have the key to his apartment. I said, 'Oh no, we're going to work this out,' and we did. I think he was only saying that to see what I was going to say.

"I had thought about leaving, but one of the things my grandmother told us was if you're going to leave, make sure that it's what you want to do and that you have no intentions of coming back. If I'd said I was going to leave Ralph, most people would have thought I was crazy, particularly most of the women I knew. He always brought his money home and gave it to me and he didn't bother me about the finances. He never asked me how much money I made from teaching and he helped with the housework.

"Communication has been the major problem in our marriage," Hattie adds. "We have better communication now. It's happened in the last five years. He's not the same person he was when we married and neither am I. We have both grown. I always expected to stay married because my grandparents were married fifty-five years. I guess now we're on our honeymoon! We finally got to it!"

"Amen," Ralph smiles.

2

OUR HISTORY WAS PARALLEL

DOROTHY AND HOLMAN EDMOND

Married July 19, 1958 · Hissop, Alabama

One Sunday evening, I was on my way to my cousin's dorm to pick up my books. I was walking alone, went around this building, and standing on the corner talking 'jive' was Holman Edmond, Jr. and his friend Robert Armstrong. As I approached he took this big apple cap off and started sweeping the ground. He said, 'Let me sweep the ground so that she can walk.' It was funny and we started laughing. From that moment we talked and he walked me to my cousin's dorm. That was the beginning," Dorothy recalls.

"During my sophomore year, I observed him more closely. One night the YWCA sponsored an international tea at the museum. Holman was president of the United Men's Congress, which was a men's group on campus. He was in the receiving line and called out my entire name. He said, 'Hello, Lee Dorothy Leonard from Hissop, Alabama.' At first, from a distance, I did not like him, because he seemed pushy and really arrogant. I thought, he's just a little bit too arrogant for me," Dorothy says.

"I met her even before we had the reception in the Carver Museum," Holman adds. "During the early part of her freshman year, there was a Student Leadership Conference. At that conference we broke into different work groups and she was in a work group with my fraternity brother, who was the group leader. She was the secretary. When we reconvened, she presented a well-written report. At Tuskegee, we called freshmen 'crabs.' I asked my fraternity brother, 'Who is that crab?' I thought, 'Give her about three more years, and let her get some of the dirt out of her skin.' She was so articulate in giving that report. She got my attention."

"The summer after my freshman year, several of us girls went to New York for summer jobs. In New York we could get jobs working for rich Caucasian people, and I could make more money there than working in Alabama. While in New York, I asked several girls what they knew about Holman Edmond. The girls that were in the choir with him said, 'He's not really a bad person, but I don't know if you want to get mixed up with him. He's really a nice person, but he's just a ladies' man.' When I returned to school a girl that was living in the same dorm with me liked him, or so I

HOLMAN AND DOROTHY

ON THEIR WEDDING DAY, JULY 11, 1958,

WITH DOROTHY'S PARENTS,

CLAUDIA AND WILLIE LEONARD.

HOLMAN, AN ARMY LIEUTENANT,

IS IN HIS DRESS UNIFORM;

DOROTHY IS NINETEEN,

BETWEEN HER SOPHOMORE AND

JUNIOR YEARS AT COLLEGE.

thought. One evening, we were talking and I mentioned Holman Edmond. She said, 'Oh, that's just my big brother. He and my brother are friends. There's nothing going on. We're just friends.'"

"I gave the appearance of being a playboy," Holman replies. "I would take one girl to the movie Friday night and I'd take another girl Saturday night. They thought I was playing, but I did not want to get serious with any one girl. If you took a girl somewhere three times, then everybody would 'plug' you. They were 'plugging' me. I wasn't the playboy they thought I was. I just couldn't afford to get serious with anybody as a sophomore or junior. This was my senior year and I could afford to get serious because I was getting a commission at the end of the year, getting my degree and going into the army. It was a strategic move," Holman explains.

"We must have talked about everything under the sun, the first time we talked," Dorothy muses, "I mean the first evening we really talked. We must have talked until ten o'clock that evening. We sat out on a bench in front of the academic building and just talked. There were so many similarities. We discovered that we both grew up on farms and in the Baptist church. Our whole life history was so parallel. The person that I would get serious about, first of all had to have a religious base. That was always important to me. Another thing this person had to have was earning potential. I did not need a lazy person in my

11

life. They may not have had money while in college, but they had to be on their way to having some earning potential. I also needed a person that had some character, who had values and some home training. Holman fit the mold that I had carved out about my ideal mate."

"I knew I liked her but I wasn't going to let any green grass grow under my feet," Holman continues. "I had intentionally not gotten too close to any young lady for three years because I couldn't afford to have a girlfriend. I was on the GI Bill and I didn't have much money. I intentionally didn't get serious. And I remember that she said someone told her that I was a playboy."

"Holman wasn't dating anybody, but I was," Dorothy continues. "I was seeing somebody at the time. He discovered I had been talking with Holman and became very jealous. One evening, this guy had the audacity to slap me. I said, 'I know you must be crazy, you must be out of your mind! Don't call me anymore until I get a signed statement from the doctor at the hospital that you are fully cured. Until then, I don't ever want to see you again.' So that was it! I never heard from him again. Holman had gotten tired of calling. My best friend in the world, Ann, said, 'Why don't you call him and apologize to him.' So I called him to let him know that I was no longer involved with this other guy. That's how it all got started."

"Long before I met Dot, I had in the back of my mind the type of person I wanted to marry," Holman says. "I never wanted a glamorous woman. I wanted a nice-looking, well-stocked, well-bred, and well-raised girl. Dot was an intelligent girl, to be nineteen. She seemed to have an intellect beyond her age. That was attractive to me."

"We were both from large families that were poor materially," Holman continues. "We were from two-parent families. She was not ashamed to invite me to come to her home because they had an outdoor toilet. That's what we had at my house. When I finished school in May of '58, I was going to give her a ring and we were going to get married, maybe Christmas '58."

"He never proposed to me, we just got married," Dorothy chimes in.

"I finished in May and went with the choir to perform at Radio City Hall for a month," Holman recalls. "I came back and worked at Tuskegee, helping them build dormitories for about five weeks. We got married in July and I went on active duty in September."

EDMOND FAMILY PICTURE
TAKEN IN 1972. FROM LEFT ARE
LORI, BYRON, DOROTHY, SANDY,
HOLMAN, AND RODERICK.

"I went back to school in September and was going into my third year," Dorothy replies. "We were doing this long-distance thing, and things just weren't clicking. I was still very much an individual—well, I still am for that matter—but I was thinking of only me. He was in New Jersey thinking 'married,' and I was thinking 'me.' We were getting into arguments over the telephone. We had nothing to build on.

"He wrote me this letter," Dorothy continues. "'I don't think this marriage is working long distance. If we are going to stay married, you need to withdraw from school and come up to New Jersey, so that we can build a marriage.' I said, 'Okay.' I don't know if I ever really discussed it in-depth with anybody. I told the dean of women that I was leaving. I valued the marriage. Therefore, I got on the train after Christmas, went to New Jersey, and that's when we first started living together, January '59.

"There was definitely a transition because he had certain ideas about marriage and so did I," Dorothy explains. "He was a very controlling person. When we got married, I was nineteen and I think subconsciously I was looking for this authority figure. Then I began to resent the controlling type. I remember our very first argument. It was about some shoes. A friend and I went to New York and stopped in Newark. I saw this pair of shoes. I love shoes. They didn't cost very much, so I bought them. When I brought them home, he went ballistic. I said 'Oh no, no, no, not my shoes!' I went to the closet, pulled out everything that I had bought since we got married and threw them on the bed."

"In 1958, a black regular army lieutenant was a rare breed," Holman chimes in. "To be frank, the army sort of dictated some of our conduct, and one of them was managing finances. I was afraid that we couldn't afford the shoes. In the military during those days a man was expected to manage his household, manage his money and manage his children. If you wanted to get put out of the army, all you had to do was start writing bad checks and let your children run wild. You didn't have that many chances. They would gladly kick you out. I had all that pressure on me and it trickled down to her."

"The hardest thing for me to do was to spend money that somebody else had earned," Dorothy explains. "It took me a long time to feel like I deserved to write a check on the money somebody else earned. It was my hang-up and something that I had to get over."

"Before we got married, we said that we would talk things out and let each other know about hurt feelings," Holman recalls. "We were married for seven years before we had an argument or a disagreement and didn't resolve it before going to sleep."

"It wasn't from my parents," Dorothy chimes in, "because my parents were at each other all the time. At Tuskegee there was a house advisor in the nurse's dorm, who pulled couples together that were dating and had sessions on Sunday afternoons. We would go to these sessions and talk about relationships. From these sessions, we decided our ground rules for fighting and they seemed to work pretty good.

"In the early stages of our marriage," Dorothy recalls, "I was not as secure or as independent as I should have been. I was content to be the one to always give in. I had to do some introspection. That's something that I've done from day one of our marriage. I guess I came into this world looking inward. One day, I sat down and looked at myself and asked, 'What is it about you that makes you think that you're so right all the time?' There were some things that I could have done, like stop bitching so much and stop being a neat freak. We grew up in the country and it was no sin to be poor, but it was a sin to be poor and dirty. It was drummed in our heads that you may not have but one pair of socks, but they need to be clean every day when you go to school. I was making myself miserable and everybody around me equally as miserable.

"It was a real shock to me, when I woke up and realized I wasn't perfect," Dorothy admits. "This is where a lot of young couples go off the deep end. They have things set up according to them—how they think, their value system—but here you are incorporating two separate value systems into something you call a marriage. It's give and take. You're not perfect all the time; you got some warts just like everybody else!

"However, you're probably with the one person who will accept you, warts and all!" Holman chimes in.

"I didn't pay that much attention to Dorothy's faults," Holman continues. "In the service, particularly in flight school, we got a lot of coaching. There were classes for wives on how to help husbands—how to support your husband, help him get through flight school, how to feed them well, and make sure they get proper rest. Somewhere along the line, Dot and I realized that we had to make time for one another. We got married July '58. She joined me in January '59 and got pregnant March '59."

"We always found time for each other," Dorothy continues. "We found time to go out to dinner, just the two of us, and we did things that did not involve the children. There were times when we sat down and talked to each other. It's not always sex, it's relating to each other. I mean just picking each others' brains and just having a good down-home conversation.

"We have always believed that it's healthy for a relationship when the lines of communication are kept open. When you spend twenty-plus years raising and educating children, if you are not careful, you will lose touch with each other. Children's activities are time consuming: scouting, little league, high school activities. You must plan time for yourselves, intentionally," Dorothy explains.

"When Holman went to Vietnam I went back to school and majored in family life education. We had four children, and I did not want to raise our children the same way I was raised, but I wanted to incorporate some of the new techniques into the old values. I was very much into family. I did not start work until the youngest child went to college. I always knew I would have a career, it was just a dream deferred as far as I was concerned.

"I'm a realist," Dorothy says. "I've tried to be realistic about this whole thing called marriage. We both realized that children don't raise themselves. Somebody has to be there to provide the day-to-day guidance. It just happened to be me, and that freed him to pursue a career. We've never had an overabundance of 'things.' A second income was not a priority when the children were at home."

"We agreed that I was going into the army to be a career person and she would go back to school and get a bachelor of science degree," Holman explains. "These were some long-range plans we made before we got married. I made lieutenant colonel. I accomplished my goals and she accomplished hers."

"One of my insecurities was that I didn't have a degree," Dorothy continues. "Every year that Holman was in Vietnam, I thought he was going to get shot and leave me with four children to raise. There was no way we could carry enough insurance to raise four kids. Once I went back to school and got the B.S. degree, I figured that it could be a springboard to do other things. I would not have to start at rock bottom if I had to go out and earn a living."

"When we first got married, we agreed to have one checking account," Holman recalls. "I was an aviator. I could take off, crash, and burn any day, so we created a plan so that she could carry on if something happened to me. We've always had one checking account, and Dot knows, right now, where every penny is. There is no false feeling that I have a stack of money over here that she doesn't know about, none of that stuff."

"The checkbook is always open," Dorothy chimes in. "Early in our marriage, when money was real, real tight, we had to watch it closer. We would discuss everything. When I needed to make a purchase, we'd discuss it."

"We have never been in competition with each other," Dorothy continues. "We did not enter this marriage in a competitive spirit. One thing I've always admired about him is he was behind me 110 percent, pushing me and encouraging me. Holman made me feel like a person in the relationship. Once I overcame my insecurities, I've never felt like an appendage. I had my own identity. I feel good about remaining a person. We have both remained individuals and encourage each other to be our best selves."

"While in the military, I was a pilot and would be away for long periods. We had to trust one another. If you want to go crazy, go around being jealous. You can lose your mind. That doesn't mean that I'll turn my woman over to another man, but if a person wants to lie or cheat they're going to do it anyway. There's nothing you can do about it."

"We've not had the jealousy problem," Dorothy continues, "but there was one woman in particular who decided that she wanted Holman Edmond. Holman's friend came to him and told him, 'You know so-and-so is really after you and she is making waves and you better talk to your wife before she picks up on this in the streets.' Holman came and talked to me and I said 'You can tell her or your friends that I have the home-field advantage.' That ended that."

"Trust is the glue that held our relationship together over the years," Holman explains. "We had our ups and downs, but we're fortunate to say we've had more ups that downs. We always prayed together and put God first in our marriage. In all marriages there will be peaks and valleys and you work to have more peaks than valleys. There will be laughter and tears, that goes with any long-term relationship. No relationship is easy. Neither of has us ever spent a night out of the house, calling ourselves mad with each other. She has never gone to another room to sleep because she was angry. We snore in each other's face, bad breath and all! We have had our arguments and I told her I'm not going anywhere."

"I told him, if we should break up, you get the children, all of them! We won't fight about that," Dorothy smiles.

"That put a damper on it," Holman laughs!

"I know I'm not perfect, but this is the person who will accept me and my imperfections," Holman explains. "Dot's my best buddy, my best friend, and she's also called my wife."

3

Becoming Whole

EVA AND VAN BIRD

Married June 29, 1946 · Chester, Pennslyvania

One of my sorority sisters introduced us. She said, 'This is my homey.' I hugged her and I hugged Van, too," Eva recalls. "That night I wrote home to my sister and told her I finally met the man that I wanted to marry. At the time I had been engaged to someone else. We had been engaged on and off since I was sixteen. He was in the service and I was wearing his ring."

"When we met we were sophomores at Fort Valley State," Van says.

"Van was cute and seemed to be a little on the shy side," Eva laughs. "I don't know what it was about him that made me want to marry him. I had dated a lot, but had not had this feeling before. I believe in soul mates. I didn't know enough about him to say it was anything else."

"Eva was sharp and witty. It became clear as we continued to talk that we shared many of the same views about life, about issues, about relationships. I would look forward to our close encounters, the moments we shared with each other. It felt like a meeting of our minds, spirits, and hearts."

"We became good friends through class discussions, which we continued after class. We would sit on the campus grounds and argue and debate issues. We were just good friends because he knew I was engaged and he had a girl back home. He didn't realize that I had already decided to marry him, so he would go to affairs with other women on campus. This made me very sad."

"I didn't just dump my girlfriend, I put her out of my mind," Van explains.

"My mama didn't like the idea of running after a man, so I had to do things to keep his attention," Eva offers. "I used to run track early in the morning and he would come outside to look at me. I would try to be one place on campus so that we could make eye contact. We really got together after I dropped him. I didn't have lunch with him any more and hardly talked with him. He started writing me letters. They were essays eight to ten pages long. He called me Sharona, an angel, and he was Beelzebub the Devil. As a result of me dropping him, he felt like he had done something wrong. I would get these essays every week. At the end of the school year, in May, we starred in a play, *The Magnificent Obsession*. He had the leading male part and I had the leading

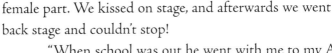

EVA BIRD;

PHOTO TAKEN DURING

EARLY YEARS OF MARRIAGE.

female part. We kissed on stage, and afterwards we went back stage and couldn't stop!

"When school was out he went with me to my Aunt Mary's and expected a continuation of that kiss," Eva says. "The bad news was that he wasn't getting any more. By then he didn't want to lose me. Van told me that he had a cousin that was getting married at nineteen. He said, 'Anybody getting married at nineteen is crazy! They're ruining their lives!' I said 'That's beautiful; marry early and have your children. That's lovely to be married and grow up together.' That's when he asked, 'Will you marry me?' He didn't realize that I had led him to that point.

"Like dummies we got on the train in Savannah looking for somebody to marry us," Eva continues. "We were eloping. It was late at night and we were asking cab drivers where we could find the justice of the peace. They misunderstood us and were telling us about a boudoir, a place to rent to have sex. We were so embarrassed we got back on the train and rode to Pennsylvania. After my mom and my family met him we were glad we didn't marry that way. When my mom met Van it was love at first sight. She saw in him what I saw. We planned to have our wedding on June 29, the last Saturday of the month. Since my mom didn't have to prepare much, she gave us a hundred dollars for a honeymoon."

"We went to Atlantic City for a whole week," Van laughs. "This was '46. We stayed there the entire week and I would go out long enough to buy food. That was our vacation, our honeymoon."

"After that we got jobs working as a couple on a golf course in Wallingford, Pennsylvania," Eva recalls. "He was the gardener and I was the maid."

"Back at school we stayed in the old army barracks, the veterans' units, the last two years," Van says. "It was interesting and fun. I worked in the dining hall. It was an adjustment, being married, but it didn't interfere with our studies. We both graduated. I was in history and political science and she was a sociology major. During the summer we got married there was a change in plans in terms of my own vocation. While walking across the golf course I had an urging to become an ordained minister. My grandparents, grandmother, and others had been moving me in that direction, which I resisted for many years. Eva affirmed it. In the fall I began preparing for theological studies and seminary."

"We were moving so fast," Eva adds. "We struggled, but we managed. Van was very smart. He wasn't the smartest one in our class, but he did come up second and I came out third. It was idyllic."

"I was the smartest; the first person cheated," Van laughs. "After graduation, we went to Chester, Pennsylvania, and by September we were in Chicago at Northwestern University."

"On the way there Van lost our last twenty dollars, so when we got there I had to do housework to earn some money. That was all the money we had."

VAN BIRD;

PHOTO TAKEN DURING

EARLY YEARS OF MARRIAGE

WHILE STUDYING TO BE AN

ORDAINED MINISTER.

"We didn't have a place to stay," Van recalls. "Eva and I were the only black couple there. At least a half dozen or so married students got together and rented a big house in Evanston, Illinois, because there wasn't housing for married students on campus."

"In order for us to stay at the house, Van had to be registered as the gardener and I the maid, so of course we didn't stay."

"Early in our marriage I had to forgive my family for lot of the ways that they raised me," Eva offers. "They were very religious. My mother was not only religious, but very spiritual. Mama believed that the wife was to be obedient to her husband. Mama was one of those old-timers that believed that God would zap you if you did something wrong. She taught us fear, like fear of water. The reason I had to forgive her was that I set out to do the opposite of almost everything she taught me except for the lasting values like being honest and being respectful. Even to this day, I have some conflict with Van due to my resistance to how I was raised. I wasn't giving him as much attention as he wanted, needed, or expected. I grew up with some rebellion in me, rebellion against my mom's strictness. Van got the brunt of that rebellion."

"I grew up in a single-parent home, so the presence of a complete family meant a lot to me. My mother and grandmother gave me the basic foundations of my values and my beliefs. Our values were some of the things that drew us together. When Eva was acting spoiled, her mother told me to spank her, which I never did," Van states. "It was frustrating, but I knew that she loved me; I never doubted that. Her mother said she was spoiled and I continued spoiling her. Years earlier while in college, she played that cat and mouse game where I'd pursue her. This continued in the early marriage."

"I didn't know how to deal with it," Eva admits. "The more he tried to control me, or so I perceived, the more I was trying to run away from it, rather than trying to reach some kind of solution. That was the biggest conflict in our marriage. When my daddy was trying to control my mama she accepted it. We were in trouble and sought counseling—we both needed it. I needed to know what to do when the "mad" love is over—the kind of passion where you pass cherries from one mouth to the other. When all of that is over that's when the work of real love begins. That's when the counselor had to tell me if you ever loved someone you definitely can learn to love them again. I needed to know that. That mad love gave way to respect for one another. It's more beautiful than it was."

"Our eyes began to open to the real meaning of love and to the real nature of relationship," Van continues. "Love is a relationship between two individuals, who in his and her own right could stand independently of the other. It reaches out. Eva and I began to understand that interdependence was necessary. The counselor said, 'I'm not trying to save your marriage. I want you to become whole, each of you to become whole.' I began to focus not on Eva or the marriage, but on my own life, my own weaknesses and strengths, and on me. I'd always had tremendous confidence in my intellectual abilities, but as a result of my experiences I was deficient with relating and understanding feelings. I had a lot of insecurities, which made me anxious in relationships. I gradually came to realize that I was able to stand on my own two feet apart from anyone else. It was reassuring knowing that I still had that bond with Eva. I wanted our marriage to work. I was determined to do whatever it took."

"He told me that after almost fifty-four years of marriage he's almost figured me out," Eva smiles. "It's not so much that I'm unpredictable. He says that I get involved in too many things with too many people. This is something that even today can get him upset. When I talk about what I'm doing he'll change the subject and won't look at me. He'll just look at the paper when he doesn't want to hear what I have to say. In the beginning, I wouldn't go someplace if he didn't want to go, but over the last eight or ten years I go anyway and he'll say, 'I miss you,' trying to make me feel guilty."

"I need, want, and depend on some kind of order and structure in my life. Stability, continuity, regularity, dependability are vital. Eva is often impulsive and changes her mind; I'm just the opposite. I'll get up and lay out my entire day in my mind and want to follow that schedule. I'm not rigid, but it frustrates me when something interrupts my schedule, particularly when I can't see any reason for it. She is very extroverted and I tend to be on the shy side, more introverted."

"He had a hard time dealing with that in the beginning, but the counselor showed me that no matter how extroverted I was, I should always consider him first. I would go to parties and dances and be all over the place, leaving him somewhere because he wasn't like that. That was a no-no."

"I believe very, very, very strongly in mutual trust, so much so that your word becomes your bond," says Van. "Come heaven or high water you do what you say you're going to do and be honest. And through all of our difficulties we were able to sustain our marriage because of the basic underlying fundamentals of honesty and truthfulness. Even if you violate the trust and don't keep your bond or your word, there's sufficient respect for each other that you share honestly, frankly, and openly."

"In 1951, we left Chicago and went to St. Thomas Episcopal Church in Philadelphia," Van continues. "In the meantime, our first daughter was born in 1949. We were in Philadelphia for two and a half years and then went to Baltimore for ten years, where we organized a congregation. Eva never fit the mold of a minister's wife. She set the terms of the relationship from the beginning. Even in seminary, she didn't get involved with the seminary wives. It was okay with me because I was a nontraditional husband."

"I've always been the way I am," Eva admits. "I never sought to conform. When black people go to an Episcopal church they think they've arrived. I came out of the Baptist church—that means that it's hard to turn a Baptist into an Episcopalian. We just wanted to have a decent home and to raise our children," Eva adds. "When we were in Baltimore, people wanted us to put our kids in these social clubs. We would ruin them by putting them in all that mess and I told them so. I wasn't too popular and they dropped me quickly. I didn't want my kids acting snotty."

"I was not extremely ambitious in terms of position, celebrity, and status," says Van. "However, I made the basic commitment that I would fundamentally provide for my family. I saw that as my responsibility. I took care of most of our bills."

"For a long time I was keeping the budget, and we had money problems. After counseling, I decided no more keeping the budget," Eva says. "After that he started keeping it. That was in '66. He saw what it was like and I have not touched it since. He's been doing well. We had money problems until I decided not to do the budget.

"I believe that the husband is head of the household in a Biblical sense," Eva continues. "The man was supposed to be the priest of the house, the teacher, the leader. He's supposed to be a good father and a good husband. Women are the influence in the house. We're the ones that keep it flowing."

"It wasn't a matter of 'I'm in charge.' In those early years, I'd wash clothes and hang them out on the line," Van admits. "The other guys would say, 'Man you aren't supposed to be washing!' I'd try to cook. Whoever was free to do it did it.

"Eva is good to me," Van continues. "She's always there when I need her. She's always there. Every year, she's given me a birthday party, and for the first twenty or thirty years of my life, growing up, I never had birthday parties."

"I couldn't have found a better man, in spite of our difficulties. They don't make them any better," Eva says affectionately.

4

THE BEST OF FRIENDS

JEAN AND LESTER SLOAN

Married October 5, 1947 · New York, New York

When I was working at the Veteran's Administration, I met Lester's sister. We got along very well," Jean begins. "We became friends. She was always saying, 'You must meet my brother; he's so cute.' At the time I had another fellow with whom I was involved. He was going away to school and we gave him a party and Les was there. After my friend went off to college, it didn't take long for us to get together. Les and I just sort of hit it off. Things happened, like death in his family. I was there to help out because I had experienced that. It just sort of progressed. My ex-boyfriend was out of the picture and Les was in."

"I had just come out of the army. I had been overseas for three and a half years and in the army for five. I thought she had great "gams" as they used to call them in those days, great legs," Les smiles. "She seemed to be a nice girl, petite and well-formed. She asked me to go to a party; she needed an escort."

"Oh yeah! I forgot about that," Jean says.

"Her other chap had gone to college. She wanted me to go, but I wouldn't go because I had to work. She was a little miffed about that. She would come around the house with my sister. We began liking each other. One day I told her, 'Look, you like me and I like you. Why don't we get married?' We started going out together and making plans. We had to save some money."

"The engagement was about ten months," says Jean. "I wasn't thinking of marriage, because I preferred to travel. Settling down to get married was not a part of my plans. What really made me take notice of him were my friends' comments. Les would come around my house and a couple of my friends saw him and said, 'Oh my God! If you don't want him give him to me!'"

"Chattel property," Les laughs.

"I began looking at him differently. We had some things in common and I let the relationship grow from there. When we married, I knew I had a man who was going to keep his commitment. I just had that feeling. I lost my parents at a very early age. It was my sister, my brother, and I. We were alone. Even though I didn't want to get married or have children, something told me that

THE SLOANS PREPARE TO
LEAVE FOR THEIR OWN LITTLE
APARTMENT FOLLOWING THEIR
WEDDING, OCTOBER 5, 1947,
NEW YORK, NEW YORK.

this was the guy for me. I've never, ever regretted it, not one day. He has been consistent from day one until this present time. They broke the mold when they made him. He's one of a kind. I feel so blessed to have had enough insight to say 'Okay, I think I had better take a chance on this one.'

"While we were courting we didn't just hold hands, we talked," Jean recalls. "I wanted to know what were his likes, his dislikes, what he found interesting. We had a big wedding. They had a bachelor party for Les. Surprisingly, he made it to the wedding!"

"At the bachelor's party I proceeded to get looped," says Les.

"I thought maybe he wouldn't show up, but he was there, waiting. They made me wait out in the car because they said it was fashionable to be late. The wedding was four o'clock on Sunday. After we left the reception, we went to our own, first little apartment. We didn't have a honeymoon," Jean laughs.

"I like to work," Les insists. "I had a few days off and went right back to work."

"Early in our marriage, any time we disagreed we sat down like two adults and discussed it and came to some conclusion; that's what we've always done," Jean continues. "What's the point in raising your voice?"

"Our marriage would appear dull by some people's standards," Les points out. "My parents had a peaceful relationship. Once in a while my mother would get a little angry, but it never developed into anything. There was consistency. My dad worked, kept out a little money for himself, and gave the rest to my mother. My mother took care of everything. I'm a person that loves figures. In those days stamps were three cents. If I bought a stamp it was on paper. After a while Jean handled the money and whatever she did with it was fine. As long as I had enough money for carfare. She used to tell me, 'Why don't you put some money in your pocket?' I didn't need any because I could get on the train or buses free, just show the shield. I was a policeman.

"If we ever had any disagreements it was about me working all the time," Les admits. "I have to stay busy. I like to learn and be busy. Sitting around the house doesn't do it for me at all. I've never made any demands on her. A lot of guys think that when you marry a woman, she's supposed to cook and all that. I can cook for myself. I can cook anything I want. I have cooked for her and the family."

"That's true, that's the way it is," Jean smiles. "He loves to eat too."

"If I want to eat, I know how to cook anything I want. I was always hanging around the kitchen when I was young. I lived with my grandmother and my mother, so I just learned. I pick up things quickly," explains Les. "I love to eat, too, so I knew I'd better learn. I'm a man, I do this; she's a woman, she does that. That's all garbage. If my wife wants to change the oil in the car, that's fine. I have a sister ten years younger than me. I changed diapers for a long time. I washed diapers, because Jean couldn't stand the smell. I'd wash them so much, my hands used to get raw. My youngest daughter received a toolbox for one of her birthdays because she likes to deal with tools. She's a programmer today. A lot of men get upset that their wives make more money than they do. I could be perfectly happy if she made a hundred thousand dollars a year. I would cook every day and the house would be clean. I'm still a man whether I'm cooking or out there fighting with the people. She's a woman. You are who you are. What you do does not define you. When we married, neither of us brought any baggage to the marriage. We had no hang-ups. We married to live with one another and to have children. Still, marriage is not all fun and games. I tend to be a loner. I enjoy being by myself and nothing bothers me."

"I am the general," Jean confesses.

"I was not going to say anything," Les laughs.

"I know how to delegate. I can give out job assignments—he never complains," Jean offers. "He'll go on and do whatever it is I need for him to do."

"I know what she's talking about. She's trying not to be such a power broker," says Les. "There's a controlling spirit in her. She likes to control things. There are times when she gets an idea and hangs onto it. It could be annoying until you understand that this is her makeup. I keep my mouth shut. To keep peace, I grin and bear it. Once in a while I might get a little testy, but not for long."

"I have to sort of step back from time to time," Jean says. "I have it in my mind how it should be, and it's not right all the time. Sometimes it's best to let a person go on and make a mistake even though you can see through certain things. Trying to hold back is difficult. I've learned patience. I'm speaking of patience with my children and my grands. I would have preferred seeing them do other things at the beginning, but the results have been satisfying. They're doing fine. Les wanted me to be home with the children because it was important during their early years. Just knowing that Mother was there. We didn't want any latchkey kids. It was a little better during our time than it is today."

"When we married, Jean was Catholic, she was raised Catholic," Les says. "I wouldn't say I was atheist, I guess maybe agnosticism would explain it best. When I was young we were never forced to go to church, but when I went I enjoyed it. My mother used to go hear Adam Powell, Sr., and take me with her. I got into Buddhism, and I thought that was great and that led me into Christianity, and gradually I became what I am now, born-again Christian. Sometimes I wonder about myself."

"Nondenominational, more Pentecostal," Jean chimes in.

"I'm not Baptist. They call them charismatics. They all got their own labels, and I don't go for labels. I serve God best by being kind as I can to others and helping others. We haven't had any conflict about religion because I went where she went to show the kids that they should go to church."

"Growing up, I was in church all day with my aunts. It was Baptist and Methodist churches. I was sent to a Catholic school where I was taught Catholicism and I immediately loved it," says Jean. "I became a Catholic. When we got ready to get married, the priest told me, 'Oh no, you're a Catholic girl, you can't be married to anybody like him.' Les wasn't a Catholic, but he was a good man, a good person. He didn't object to the children being brought up as Catholics. We could not get married in front of the altar because Les wasn't Catholic."

"I pray and we pray together when we have a specific problem," Les admits. "In the Bible, Jesus said to go into your closet and speak to your Father. He didn't say anything about taking somebody with you. We didn't have any problems or we handled them as they arose."

"People don't believe this but it's true," says Jean. "We don't have problems."

"Not even monetary differences," Les points out.

LESTER HAVING FUN AT
JONES BEACH ON LONG ISLAND,
NEW YORK, WITH THE CHILDREN
ELLEN, MARTIN, AND GEOFFREY,
IN 1954.

"We believe in putting everything together. We always had joint accounts," Jean explains. "It's always been together."

"I realized she had the talent to do that, so she did it. She was the manager of a bank. Money had never made a great impact on me. If I have enough to eat and something to wear, I'm fine."

"People swore up and down that Les was taking graft," Jean adds. He has never taken one quarter from anybody, at any time, doing anything. He worked, got his money, and came home with his salary. We were not ones to buy impulsively. We saved towards whatever we wanted. Whatever we decided to get we would have saved for it before we ventured off to buy. We've tried to be good stewards of our money. We tried to teach this to our children, too. We've talked to our children about our disagreements, so that they know that we have disagreed. As adults, we used our minds to settle things. It can be done in a nice way."

"One of my favorite things to say is, you must accept human beings as they are if you're going have any kind of relationship," says Les. "You either accept them or you don't. If you don't accept them, then don't be bothered with them, whether it's business, marriage, or playing. Leave them alone."

"The key is listening," Jean smiles.

"People will tell you in little ways who they are if you listen," Les agrees.

"We've always impressed that upon our children as they were finding friends," Jean continues. "It doesn't take long for you to know what type of person this is if you listen."

"God, in His wisdom, with the billions of people, made no two alike," Les explains. "There's a reason for this. We must learn to accept each other. If you don't like something they're doing, leave them alone. After a certain age, they will not change."

"That's why we talked extensively before we got married." Jean says. "I even asked him was there was any insanity in his family. It was important for me to know. There's going to be some things about the other person that you don't particularly like, but you must figure out if you can live with it, because you're not going to change them. We made certain that we understood one another from the beginning. We constantly communicate. We've learned to listen carefully to what the other is saying. If there are some changes that need to come about it should be something that both are well aware of. I've learned that I can't keep things to myself and feel as though he will eventually understand what is on my mind. I have to speak openly about everything at all times."

"That's all a part of growing up," Les offers. "You grow, you listen, and you learn. If you want to be child, then be a child, but don't get married. There are people who are sixty who have not grown up. Growing up means you accept conditions as they are and then do the best you can with them. Don't denigrate or judge. It's as simple as that—grow up. I never expected it to be anything but a long-lasting marriage if I was in it. Jean will always be there for me. It's unexplainable. We get along and we've always gotten along, no problems. There's nothing she could do that would upset me, nothing."

"There's not a day that passes that Les doesn't show me love. I can see his car coming and my heart skips a beat. I've never lost that feeling that I had for him when we first got married. He's a very thoughtful person. We don't kiss or slobber over each other every day, but there is something he does. He'll get up in the morning and the first thing out of his mouth, after saying good morning, is 'What can I do for you? What should we do today? Can I make breakfast?' He starts the day that way. It's being in his company. There is something about him that makes my day. I can't envision a day without him. We are the best of friends."

5
STRAIGHT UP AND FOR REAL

BETTYE AND WILLIAM BOZEMAN

Married August 23, 1969 · Greenville, Alabama

I'd just gotten out of high school and was working at a shoe store," Willie begins. "They were beginning to integrate the city and I was working at Maryland Shoes as a shoe salesman and stock boy. This particular day a lady, who was looking for sandals, came in the lobby. She picked up the sandals she wanted and tried them on and said, 'Oh I like this pair, I'll buy them.' I wrote the ticket for the sale and took it to the cashier. I looked at her and asked, 'Where do you live?' She said, 'I'm in school at Alabama State. I'm going home for the summer.' I asked for her phone number and she gave it to me. She left and I didn't see her for about a year or so. One day on my way home on the bus, I saw her. I asked, 'Do you remember me?' She said, 'No.' I took out the piece of paper where she had written her name and number on the paper and asked, 'Is this your writing?'"

"I remember the store incident vividly," Bettye adds. "When I got ready to pay for the sandals, I didn't have enough money to pay the tax. Willie said, 'No problem, I'll take care of the tax for you.' I didn't think much about it at the time, but I did think that gesture was very nice. I went home for the summer and didn't hear from him until the next year when I saw him on the bus. I remembered him, but didn't let on until he pulled out the piece of paper. Thereafter, I saw him more regularly on the bus as I was going from school to my aunt's house."

"I had forgotten about the tax I paid; there was something about this lady that got me going. She weighed about 115 pounds and was neat and clean. I could tell that she hadn't been throwing herself away. Bettye was straight up and for real," Willie states adamantly. "That got me! She hadn't been out there running the streets, clubbing, and all that kind of stuff. She had a good future ahead of her and was looking forward to a good life, maybe a family life."

"Willie would stare at me," Bettye says. "One of my friends said, 'I think he likes you a lot. Don't you see how he stares?' I hadn't noticed."

"She had forgotten me. She probably remembered the face because she always thought I dressed like a playboy, always dressing in a suit. I had decided to wait until the time was right to approach her, to let it happen," Willie says.

WILLIE AND BETTYE
ON THEIR WEDDING DAY,
AUGUST 23, 1969,
GREENVILLE, ALABAMA.

"He came on like a playboy. I knew I did not want anybody like that in my life," Bettye admits. Willie had a mixed personality. He was a very outgoing person, who doesn't ever meet any strangers. The first time he called me, I told him I was busy and he called again. The second time, I told him I was going home for the weekend, and the third time, I told him he could come over. He didn't understand why I was putting him off for so long. He said, 'You were about to miss out on your opportunity with me, because I was not going to call anymore.' The reason I didn't give him a date when he called was because he seemed so cool, as if when he asked for a date I'd readily say yes and be so excited. After that, we started talking consistently, and then he was drafted into the army. When this happened I realized that I cared more about him than I had admitted."

"We dated for about three years and then I went overseas," Willie says. "It was the Vietnam war."

"When he went into the service we communicated back and forth," says Bettye. "While he was away I met other friends on campus, another male. It was not over between us, I was just talking to somebody else. This guy was a friend, not a close friend."

"I was in St. Louis and had a weekend leave, so I decided to come home. I went to see her and I had on my military uniform. Being excited, I ran all the way to her house. I knocked on her door. She said come in.

We're sitting on the sofa talking and this guy walks to the back of the house. Finally he walks in and says, 'Oh, excuse me, are you ready to go?' I look at her and she looks at the guy. I had just got out of combat training and was ready to tear a guy up, but you must think before you jump. Bettye sat there and eventually said, 'I'm not going anyplace.' He went out the door. I guess they were going to double date, because another guy and his girlfriend were outside."

"It was not a planned date," Bettye explains. "He would normally call before coming over, but my aunt was on the phone that particular afternoon, so he just proceeded to come over. He had made Kappa that day and decided they would get together. Nothing was planned."

"Prior to all of this we had planned to get married. Our plans changed when I was drafted," says Willie. "I loved her and she loved me."

"After I graduated from college, I spent my first year working in Alabama," says Bettye. "We had been writing each other while he was away, but when he came home on furlough and saw me talking to somebody else, he said, 'I thought about giving you rings earlier. After what I've seen—Oh no! If we're meant for each other you'll be here when I get back.' He proceeded with his duties. I really didn't think anything of it. When I finished high school, I was 'in love' with this other guy. He broke my heart to the point that I was totally hurt and didn't trust guys. I was completely through with all of them. It took me a long time to trust another one.

"When I met Willie I didn't know where he was coming from. Although he cared a lot for me before he went into the service, I wasn't really sure about him. My mother said, 'Willie seems to be a very nice young man. You've been hurt and it seems like you're not going to get yourself together to the point that you will ever accept anybody. You're going to have to get yourself together or else you're going to miss out.' I told her he's a big guy and I've never dated a big guy like this before.

"She said, 'He's a good man; I don't see why you look at that.' I was fooling myself by not letting on that I really cared for him. I was trying to fight it but deep down inside I cared a lot for him. I was in love with Willie. When he came home on furlough and saw me with someone else he was very disappointed. We continued to communicate and talk about getting married in the summer. It was the most exciting part of my life when I knew he was home for good."

"I dated other women, but it wasn't serious," says Willie. "We went on picnics or met at the club, a dance, or a house party. We just had fun. When I got out of the service, some of the women thought that I ought to get married to them. I had a lot of admirers, but I wasn't serious about any of them."

"When Willie and I first started dating seriously, my father said, 'He seems to be a very nice guy, but he appears like he wouldn't lift a hand to do too much of anything.' My mother thought he was wonderful. When Willie went to the Army and came back, my dad's perception of him changed. He said, 'He's a wonderful guy. The Army has really changed him. I honestly feel that he will make you a very good husband.'"

"I always liked to look neat," Willie says. "I wore suits and ties all the time, so most people had a perception that I'm not going to work or dig ditches. They had it all wrong. My grandfather showed us how to dig potatoes and set out potato slips. My grandmother taught us how to cook. When I got married I didn't tell Bettye I knew how to cook. If she got sick or she couldn't do, then it was time for me to do. My dad did the same thing. We were taught the basics coming up. We didn't show them until you get to a point that you must use them.

"Finally, I told my parents that I'm ready to get married," Willie continues. "They never took me seriously about anything. I told them I was bringing her by that afternoon. The house was in a shambles, books here, books there, books everywhere. When I got back that afternoon they had straightened up; they were ready for us. I said we're going to get married and would like for you (my dad was a minister) to perform the ceremony. My dad thought that Bettye was real nice, but he was always on the go so he didn't see much of her. My mother always thought a lot of her. She said, 'She doesn't call you like these other girls. With these other girls the phone rings off the hook. She doesn't call you, I like that.' Bettye's not going to call me, I call her.

"After we got married I had to explain to my mother that I had a wife now," Willie points out. I said 'Look, sweetheart, I'm getting ready to get married.' She said, 'You ought to buy us a house.' I said 'Honey, if I buy a house for you and Dad, what am I going to do for my wife?' I had to talk straight about that. I couldn't do for her and then neglect my wife. My mother and I were close,

WILLIE WITH DAUGHTER TESHA,

AS A TWO-YEAR OLD

DURING THE MID-1970S.

real close. If I was out on a date I'd call back and say hello. That was letting her know that I cared, that I loved her. I do my wife the same way. But I had to tell her right up front. I said, 'I'm not going to be able to do the things I used to do. I have to take care of my wife.' She accepted it, though she didn't want to. She didn't say it, but I could see it by the expression on her face. Our bond was still good; she loved Bettye just like she did me."

"The first five years were like peaches and cream," Bettye smiles. "We didn't have our daughter until after five years, so that gave us a lot of time to spend together and to really learn each other better. I found out that to make a marriage work you had to have open communication. If there was a disagreement about something, you could not just hold it in. Sometimes men do this. We would sit down and I'd say, 'What's wrong? Come on, open up, tell me, because I can tell something is wrong.' And then I'd ask him what makes him happy. Once he discussed it and let me know what makes him happy, I tried my best to do it and he did the same for me. It works. There must be an open line of communication. Any time two people spend time together, differences will arise. If one is upset, then obviously that's not a good time to talk—wait until you cool down. Find out what has caused the problem and what is the best way to prevent it from happening again."

"My dad was a minister and was one of the top ministers in the state of Alabama," says Willie. "He was on the go quite a bit and away from his family. I decided that the best thing to be a good husband is to stay with your family. Our family always ate together on weekends. We'd all sit down and have prayer. We talked about daily business and were taught to always treat people nice.

"The first thing that really bothered my manhood was the finances," Willie continues. "I liked to keep money in my pocket. After being paid I would come home and decide what we're going to do for the house. There wasn't any budget. Bettye brought home a budget and said, 'We're going to have to do something about this money. We must have a budget.' I said okay, but it bothered me, because it meant that I had to put all the money up front. I had to show it all. That is very important. A lot of people keep a lot of secrets—that's not good. I put the money up, so she would know what we had to work with. I didn't have any girlfriend's money or party money, it's all there. That's tough for a man to do. None of my money is going to Jean or Judy or whomever. I'm not out there. When you're honest, that strengthens the family.

"With everything else I was adjustable. If I had to eat chicken three times a day, three days a week it wouldn't bother me," Willie offers. "A black man carries a big stick. The lady has to slave, to cook, and all this. A lot of people believe that; I don't. I knew how to cook, but during our first five years I didn't cook. When she got sick, that's when she learned I could cook."

"He's been cooking ever since, whether I'm sick or not," Bettye chimes in.

"She's working and it seems like her job has gotten tough, so I clean up, vacuum, wash," Willie says. "I bet she couldn't tell you the last time she washed clothes."

"Some weekends I come in and say, 'Honey, I'm dead tired, I need rest,'" Bettye continues. "He says, 'Listen, don't you worry about anything because I got it.' That's from laundry to cleaning the bathroom to cooking or whatever else needs to be done."

"In our early marriage, I thought that a man would be weak doing those kinds of things—then I got smart," Willie admits. "I realized that it was just an ego thing. The man's in control. He's got money in his pocket, he makes the money, he pays the bills—that's a myth of power, you know. I believe if you got a little God in your heart it helps. It worked for me."

"Sometimes I get a bit carried away, impatient," Bettye offers. "When we get ready to go out of town I get a bit anxious and excited to the point of being pushy. He has never liked that. I can hardly wait, let's leave, let's go now, and you're moving a bit too slow. When it first happened I could tell he didn't like it. He would stop and say, 'Honey, why are you acting this way?' This was during the time he was working in the shoe store and working late hours. I did not realize that he was tired and that probably added to his moving a bit slower than usual. I had been home all day. I had packed and was ready to go. When we first got married I had to put that in check. I've learned to kind of settle down."

"I'm friendly. Sometimes when I'm nice to people, people take me the wrong way, particularly women," Willie explains. "We could be together and I'll introduce her as my wife. Even some of her friends take my friendliness the wrong way. They think that I'm the kind of guy that will fly the coop. In church it's the same way. It's my personality and I'm that way all the time. I got it from my mother. I don't meet any strangers. It's hard for me to get angry, but if I do I'm kind of hard to handle."

"When we got married I could never tell when he would be angry. He would look the same, a straight face. It frightened me," Bettye admits. "Now I can detect it right away."

"We don't agree on everything," Willie admits. "She thinks I spend too much time in church. Church affairs take up a lot of time. Because of this, I'm away. She likes me close to her."

"Not here all the time, but at least give me some time," Bettye insists. "I need my time too. The most challenging aspect of our marriage is Willie's friendly, outgoing personality. Sometimes it puts me in a bad predicament, where I've had to talk to some women. They disregard me and deal with him oftentimes and I have to let them know I am his wife."

"I thought they should know because I'm not the type of person that's going to engage in a long conversation." Willie adds. "Women try to get your attention and then they want to get in the middle of your family life. Long as you keep them out of that you're all right, but if you ever let them get into that they can be corruptive. A lot of people are jealous."

"During the time I was pregnant, I received a telephone call from a lady. She said, 'May I speak with Willie Bozeman, please?' She didn't tell me who she was; however, she proceeded to tell me that they had spent time in the park. She went on and elaborated about it. I said, 'Hold on a moment, let me get him.' I put him on the phone and I got on the other phone and listened. I forgot what she said, but I went completely off. I was pregnant. Willie held me that entire night and had tears running down his face trying to convince me that it was nothing. All I could see was he was trying to tell me something when he was doing something else behind my back. We talked and he didn't convince me that night. That was a really big disappointment, since we've been married. I had a good pregnancy but had some mixed emotions. I felt I was the ugliest thing walking around. Willie reassured me that I was pretty and special."

"I'd rather not hurt anybody's feelings," Willie explains. "People use the church for a whole lot of other stuff. A lot of ladies get in the church for a lot of other things than the Lord's business."

"I enjoy it when he spends valued time with me, and when he's honest," Bettye offers.

"A lot of attention," Willie chimes in.

"Yes! A lot of attention, not just saying he loves me, but actually showing it," Bettye states. "Like taking part in household chores, particularly when I'm out working eight hours a day. He shows me this commitment when he gets up every day and goes to work, brings the money home, and we pool it together. He provides for the family, making sure everything is moving smoothly."

"I feel loved when my good works are appreciated," Willie smiles. "Bettye lets me know by expressing it in some way. It's a strange thing; the two of us are basically on the same level. During the first five years we had an adjustment, but now we both almost think alike."

"When I'm upset, he doesn't go around as though nothing is going on. When I'm upset, he's upset. It bothers him as well—not to the extent it does me, but he's concerned. I look at Willie as being my arm and shield, one that I can embrace, depend upon, and to whom I can talk about anything."

"She's been a pillar of love for thirty years, and I've tried to do my best as a black man to respect her and love my family," Willie beams.

6
Believing in a Being
Greater than Ourselves

IRENE AND JOSEPH YARBROUGH

Married August 6, 1955 · Richmond, Virginia

Freshman year I used to sit behind the basketball team and tease Joe about sitting on the bench and never playing," Irene laughs affectionately. "We were always teasing each other about him sitting on the bench."

"She was looking at my legs," Joseph beams.

"Meeting Joe our freshman year in college stood out in my mind because he looked so over-whelmed seeing all those black women. He and a friend of his came to the gym, stood, and stared at all the black women as if to say, this is heaven. I'd been in a segregated system, so Virginia Union was nothing new. He had been in a mostly integrated system."

"That's true, because I had never seen so many good-looking black women in one spot," Joseph agrees. "It was a revelation to me, especially the different complexions and all the different styles of dress. I'd never had a black teacher until I went to Virginia Union. It was really a different sort of world and I had never lived in a completely segregated neighborhood."

"I remember him of all the fellows I saw freshman year, but we really didn't start talking until we were sophomores. I had a boyfriend that was a local boy from Richmond. He was not in college. I had only two boyfriends in my experience when I started seeing Joe. When we finally got together he wanted to come visit me at my home. My father said, 'I don't want those fellas from Virginia Union coming to my house, because they're coming to get a meal. I don't like it when that's all they have on their mind.' After that I was so reluctant to bring anybody home."

"I was fascinated," Joseph exclaims. "The people were very open and everybody spoke to each other. I liked the friendliness. A South Carolinian grandmother raised me like a southerner. I was not a typical northerner, because I always answered my elders by 'Yes, sir' and 'No, ma'am.' In college all the southerners thought I was from the South because of the way I communicated."

"He looked innocent, nice, respectful. He wasn't trying to be a playboy. He had the kinds of qualities I would want in man, respectful of women. Even sitting on the bench he was kind and nice. Nice is such a little word, but it means a lot.

"On our first date I wore a blue velvet dress," Irene beams. "I remember telling a friend that I hadn't a thing to wear. She offered to let me wear her blue velvet dress. I never borrowed clothes from anybody, but she insisted. I wore it and Joe just loved that dress! The one thing I borrowed in my life, Joe would ask, 'When are you going to wear that blue velvet dress again?'"

"Her smile—she had the greatest smile. She was friendly, gracious, and southern belle-ish; that made an impression on me. That smile got me, she was the kind of person that you'd want to talk to, plus she was a good student. Academics were important to me. We had similar goals. She was a scholarship student and I liked talking with her. The first impact she had on me was physical; after the initial attraction other qualities grew."

"We did what people typically did during those times. We met on campus, sometimes had lunch together, and took classes together. Math and science were my subjects. Joe was the writer. In the philosophy class we were together. We had to write our philosophy of life. After talking with Joe about my philosophy of life, he helped me write it. I got an "A+" and he got a "C." The professor said, 'Wow, I can't believe you, as a math scientist, would have these beliefs.' He was a minister and was surprised that I believed in God and heaven."

"Her responses were such stereotypical responses. That's what burned me up. The professor wasn't showing

JOSEPH AND IRENE
CUT THEIR WEDDING CAKE,
AUGUST 6, 1955,
RICHMOND, VIRGINIA.

any objectivity, no depth of understanding. Because Irene was a scientist he gave her more credit for having the beliefs she did."

"By this time my father was not well," says Irene. "He had several strokes and, being a private man, he didn't talk much."

"Irene's dad looked at me suspiciously, but he didn't say anything negative about me."

"Around this time Joe and I had a big falling out. He stood me up. One evening I took the trolley to campus and Joe was supposed to meet me on the corner. When I got there, Joe was nowhere in sight. I waited and waited."

"Two minutes!" Joseph exclaims.

"I took the trolley and went back home. He messed up and we weren't talking for a while."

"I was talking, but you weren't talking to me," Joe points out. "I would try to talk, but she didn't want to discuss the issue. I was trying to bring out things to deal with them. Irene would do that quiet treatment thing, where she would refuse to respond. Suppression is how she dealt with a lot of things."

"Only back then and when we first got married," Irene points out. "When things weren't good I'd go quiet. Now I talk too much and let everything out."

"That's for sure," Joseph laughs.

"Most of the time when we had our spats, somebody was interfering in our relationship," Irene recalls. "When Joe saw both of my old boyfriends, he playfully said, 'Gee, I don't have any competition. Is that what I have to deal with?' I had two other boyfriends before Joe and Joe felt like he was the best."

"Girlfriends? I didn't have many because I was into athletics. Basketball, football, and working took up my time, so I didn't have a social life. Dancing, I didn't know how. My mother taught me before I went to my senior high prom. I'm a good ballroom dancer, but I didn't do the jitterbug. I didn't do a lot of dancing because I didn't date much. That's why it was such a revelation to me to see so many attractive women. I didn't have any steady girl. If they started to get close or serious I would want to leave; I couldn't lead anybody on in a relationship unless I was committed to it. Guys would say, 'Oh Joe, tell them anything, they'll believe it.' I couldn't do it. I'm not going to tell you something I don't feel. My grandmother, who was a very religious woman, was very influential in my life. She would always talk about social justice, being from the South. And it was important to be loyal, committed, and truthful.

"Irene was the first woman that I was committed to," Joe continues. "I wanted to be committed to Irene. We graduated in '54 and married in '55."

"My first teaching job was in Winston-Salem, North Carolina, and Joe went to graduate school at Atlanta University."

"We didn't have enough money to travel back and forth on weekends. Atlanta was a good distance from Winston-Salem," says Joe. "While we were away from each other, Irene was able to save her money. She gave it to her mother to pay for the wedding."

THE YARBROUGH FAMILY
IN THE MID-1970S: IRENE, LISA,
AND JOE ON THE SOFA; JULIE
AND AARON IN FRONT.

"Dad died while I was in college, and my mom had four children. I was the oldest. I wanted to do something for Mom the year before I got married. So, the first year I worked I saved the money. In 1954—it seems like such a little bit now—but I was making eighteen hundred dollars per year. I couldn't believe I saved as much as I did."

"A thousand dollars!" Joe chimes in. "I didn't have any money."

"My rent was thirty-five dollars a month and the school was a block from where I lived. It was unbelievable. I didn't have a car. The wedding was at my grandmother's house and didn't cost the entire thousand dollars. As you can see, my wedding was not nearly as expensive as weddings are today. From the beginning, we came to the marriage with nothing except a job. We worked together and pooled our money. We put our money in one pot. It has worked beautifully."

"I married a mathematician who basically takes care of the books," Joe grins.

"Joe and I remained apart for the first year of our marriage. I taught in Winston-Salem for another year."

"Then I was drafted."

"By this time we had moved to Philadelphia and were staying with his mother and father. I continued to stay with them while he was in the service. Right away I got a job teaching in Camden, New Jersey. As soon as I got out of school I went to visit Joe where he was stationed, in Georgia. While I was there he said, 'You're not going back to Camden next year to teach. You're going stay here with me.' I didn't want to give up my job. I mean, I live to work. This was a conflict because I hadn't planned to give up my job. But I did and stayed with him. Maybe I prayed. Here I have a job and have to give it up in a sense to hold my marriage together. Couples today say, 'I can't, I don't want to do that,' but it worked out because I ended up getting a job teaching math."

"In making those decisions we didn't think of career first," Joseph admits. "We thought of our marriage first, and our marriage was more important than the career. The reality is, status and money are only the artificial aspects of a real relationship."

"There was another instance I had to put my career on hold for the betterment of our marriage," Irene offers. "After coming back to Philadelphia, I got a job at the Philadelphia High

School for Girls, which was a really excellent job. It was wonderful and I had a good time teaching. Because Joe got a job in Washington, D.C., I was there only one year. It was quite a promotion for him and we said, 'What are we going to do?' We decided he was going to commute. He'd come home on the weekends. After a month he said, 'I can't live like this; either you're going to come to Washington or I'm giving up the job.'"

"I had never worked in a political environment like the national government," admits Joe. "The guy that hired me was an assistant secretary to the Department of Health, Education, and Welfare under the Nixon administration. I had been a community organizer working on the street. With politics, I was a complete novice. Psychologically, it made an impact on me and I didn't have anyone I could talk to or be with after work. On the job there were so many cutthroat political things going on. People would say and do anything. All they wanted was to be in the shadow of an elected official.

"Many of them were Princeton and Yale graduates," says Joe. "Here I was coming from a small black school and they are having to report to me. They didn't like that. These were all lawyer types and this black man was not acceptable to them as their supervisor. As a result of the job, I discovered other aspects of my own academic capacity. Don't forget this was 1972. Even though things had changed in America, the pressures on African Americans were still fairly great, particularly at that level. I felt I needed my family with me for support."

"Again, I gave up my job. I did it for Joe and for the marriage. I put my career on the back burner to be with him. I was disappointed that I had to leave that school. At the same time, I knew that it was valuable for our relationship and the family, so I didn't go with a pout or anything. After a year he was able to get a transfer to the regional office in Philadelphia and I began teaching again. Not at the same school, but at a newly opened school. So everything worked out."

"I just thought she would come. I felt that if I was there, and our marriage was the important thing, she would come. I must admit I didn't think that much about her side of it. I could have been more considerate. I'm a person that has been easily focused on what I wanted to achieve and sometimes I don't take into consideration other peoples' desires. I have always been the sort of person

49

that, if things didn't go right, I would get another job. I was only able to do that because of my wife, who always worked and had a job while I moved from job to job. I remember quitting a job because I felt that folks weren't treated right. I left and went out and got a government grant to set up a program. In the interim we didn't have any money coming in."

"A baby was coming and I thought 'Oh no,'" recalls Irene. "He comes home and says, 'I told them I'm going to leave. It's just ridiculous how they're treating people. I'm going to leave in two months.' You sure you want to do this? He said 'Yes.' I was really concerned because he didn't have another job—he just quit."

"Remember, I went on unemployment," Joe recalls with a smile.

"Those were not easy times and I had to pray and talk to myself about him a lot. Why did Joe do that? But we made it and things stayed solid. In any marriage there are going to be valleys and things will turn out okay. He quit for a noble cause. There's no perfect mate and if you're looking for a perfect mate you're going to have trouble. Decide what values you can live with and those you can't, and if you can't live with the other person's values, don't marry."

"I would say we're co-bosses; we mutually make decisions," Joe offers.

"It is fifty-five to forty-five, with Joe being the fifty-five and me being the forty-five. It's my problem. I take after my mother. My father was the dominant person in our family as it was in many traditional families. My mother was the homemaker who took care of the house and children. With my father and mother it was probably eighty-five to fifteen. When there was going to be the purchase of a sofa or refrigerator, he would bring them home and give them to my mother as a Christmas or birthday present. He was making all the decisions. Because of my upbringing, I probably thought of the woman being under the husband. There was a little bit of that in me. I tease Joe because it took me forty years to find out he didn't know everything. Because most of the time whatever he said I assumed he was right, because that's the way I looked at my father. My personality's a little different now. 'No, Joe, uh-uh, sorry. You don't know that.' Because if he said it was green, and I thought it was blue, I would say okay it must be green."

"I don't think it was quite that dramatic," Joe says.

"No, no, no, not quite that bad. Decisions relating to the children, we talked to each other about it," Irene points out. "If there was a conflict, we resolved it away from the children. Joe listened—my father didn't. The children thought I was being submissive because they didn't know the process we went through."

"I was the disciplinarian, so the kids saw me as the person that was giving the final word," says Joe.

"Joe has a strong personality. It's moderate and easy to deal with most of the time. But when the stubbornness comes out, he can't be budged. If I tell him to turn right, he may turn left. I'll say 'When I tell you to turn right, you turn right.' He doesn't pay me any attention! When I tell him rather than ask him, that strong personality comes out."

"As Irene has gotten older she belabors things a little more. She displays a little anxiety and I try to calm her down. She likes to worry and that worries me because I can't seem to soothe her."

"It's part of me, and it has always been there," Irene insists. I'm a 'what if' person. It's sort of like math. Sometimes it can be good to think ahead, thinking through the possibilities that could happen and how to avoid them."

"Impending doom complex," Joe laughs affectionately. "I'm always calm, but Irene would like for me to be more attentive. I'm not the touchy-feely type. I don't show as much affection openly as I should. I have a tendency to show it by buying expensive gifts. I'm not physically expressive in terms of my feelings, my romantic feelings."

"I'd like Joe to be more touchy, not in a sexual way. When we go to the movies we hold hands. We kiss each other good-bye when we're going to work. I would like it to be a little bit more touchy that doesn't lead to any sexual thing. After forty-four years of marriage I still enjoy being with Joe. We get out in the morning and go for a morning walk and enjoy nature and feel good being together. I'm happy to see him walking across the yard coming home."

"It's been the love and support I've gotten from Irene. In my career, my belief system, or the stands I've taken, she's never knocked me down. Believing in a Being greater than ourselves has the been the foundation upon which we built our marriage."

7
Building a Marriage

A U R E T H A   A N D   J E T H R O   E N G L I S H

Married November 24, 1937 · Atlanta, Georgia

At Ebenezer Baptist Church, Fellowship Hall, me and some girls were sitting over on one side of the church and the boys on the other. We had a social one night, down at the church, for members who had recently joined the church. Jethro came over to where we were and threw his cap in my lap. I thought, 'Wonder what's the matter with him?' Auretha smiles. "In those days if a young man threw his cap in a lady's lap and she didn't throw it back that meant everything was all right."

"She seemed to be the kind that I liked," Jethro smiles. "She was kind of lively and very talkative. She did a lot of good things. That was in 1932."

"I kept the cap," Auretha beams. "In watching him at church, he always seemed to be such a nice fella. He was a junior deacon. He wasn't loud or rowdy. He was kind of soft, you could see it in his eyes. When the social was over, he asked me if he could walk me home and I said, 'Yeah, I don't care.' We started courting from that day on. His father was my favorite deacon. He was a little fat, chubby man and just as friendly as he could be. His father impressed me."

"My mother died when I was three years old," Jethro says. "My daddy wasn't a well-trained man, he worked at night as a cook. My old man was working, working, working trying to take care of me, my sister, and my stepmother. I could see the strain on my daddy trying to take care of us. I stopped school to help out and started working. I had four jobs at one time. I quit school, so my sister could go to college. I helped my daddy send my sister to college. While I was working, I was looking for somebody I could trust, somebody I could love, and somebody I could build a life with, like I thought it was supposed to be, according to my daddy. He was a Christian man with morals and straight living. He'd pray all the time but things weren't going so well in our house. I said, 'When I get me a wife we going to do better that that.'"

"When we first met I was eighteen," Auretha recalls. "I wanted to finish school. When I finished Washington High in 1935, we married in 1937. We did some serious courting from '35 to '37.

53

Before then we were playing around, social courting. I had another boyfriend. He wasn't like a real boyfriend. He was more like an acquaintance; it wasn't a serious thing."

"I had other girlfriends too. It was a time in my life for just playing. You had your main girl, and you had other girls that would go to the dances with you. I went to dances with Auretha too. I'd ask her to go to the show and she would always say, 'I don't care,' Jethro says. "She would always give me that, 'I don't care.' That was always my invitation and I took that to be serious. I said, 'I'd like to come by and take you to the show. Would you like to go to the show?' The same, 'I don't care.' It's a funny thing about her, the first time I started going to get her, she was sitting up there in the house. She wasn't ready to go to no show. I said, 'I told you I'd be here.' It was two or three times after that, before she told me that she didn't want nobody to stand her up. After she found out that I was truly reliable, she'd be ready every time I told her I'd be there."

"One time, I remember when I was sick, Jethro used to bring me grapes every time he would come to see me. After that, one of my friends told me, she said, 'You going to marry Jethro.' I said, 'I bet I don't.' We kept on dating and got engaged.

"We got married at my mother's house," says Auretha. "She had it all decorated and the lady next door made flower arrangements. The choir came from church."

"The night we married, my buddy, who would be my best man, was running late," Jethro adds. "He had to get his suit. We got there just in time for prayer meeting. We had prayer meeting before the wedding."

"I was happy about it," Auretha laughs. "We married on my birthday. I wasn't nervous, I was just waiting on the time because he had asked me to marry him twice before and I kept saying no. After I finished high school I wanted to work a while. We kept courting. The next year, it got a little more serious. He asked me to marry him again, and I said, 'Let's wait a little longer.' When he asked me the third time, I said, 'Yeah!'"

"When it was over we put the presents aside and the honeymoon began," Auretha continues. "Jethro had a friend that worked for an undertaker. They had big black limousines, so he took us across town to my friend's house and we stayed there for a good while. After a while we wanted to go

AURETHA AND JETHRO
WITH THEIR TWO CHILDREN—
LAURA, TWO YEARS OLD,
AND RONALD, FOUR—
IN ATLANTA, GEORGIA, 1946.

home, so we left her house and came on back home. We rode from one side of town to the other, that was our honeymoon. Before we got married, Jethro rented an apartment and furnished it. My mother made the curtains and the draperies so that the night we married we had our furniture and everything. The house was already set up. When we came back from 'cross town, he picked me up and took me across the threshold into the house. It was beautiful."

"When we married, I didn't know nothing," Jethro admits. "All I knew was we wanted to build a happy marriage and we wanted to go by what the preacher said. Rev. King said, 'Until death do we part.' He looked straight at me and that thing hung right there and still does. To have and to hold in sickness and in health, that was the thing that really stuck with me. We were trying to build a marriage. I'm different, she's different, but we got to make our lives a mutual affair. She likes some things; I like some things. I know what she likes; she knows what I like. She knows what I don't like, and I know what she don't like. We don't bother that stuff, that's off limits. That's the way you do it."

"Any time we had an argument," Auretha continues, "I'm talking and he's talking. He can't hear what I'm saying and I can't hear what he's saying. I'd go to the bathroom and close the door and stay. I'd take a bath and by the time I stayed in there long enough and came out it'd all be over. We have never had a disagreement that was so bad that I'd say, 'I'm going back home.' I have never wanted to go back home and Jethro has never treated me to the point where I think this was a mistake and I want to go back home.

"My mother told me," Auretha continues, "'You are going to get married, and be sure you love who you marry. I don't want nobody picking on you, and if you marry anybody and they want to pick on you, you come on back home. You tell them you coming back home where he found you.' I don't think you should have any bickering, fussing and fighting."

"Her mother told me that if she needs a whipping, send her home to me, because I know how to whip," Jethro offers. "It was her way of saying, don't be hitting on my daughter."

"Mama said, 'When you get a husband you should be able to reason things out together. And if ya'll can't reason things out together, just hush.' I had a loving mother and grandmother who instilled the facts of life in me," adds Auretha. "My grandmother was like another mother of his. She felt like he was her child."

"I prided myself to hang around good folks," Jethro chimes in. "Her grandmother was a staunch Christian lady and she got out there and did things for the church. Her mother called me 'Happy Dan,'

AURETHA AND JETHRO SHARE A HAPPY MOMENT IN 1959, TWENTY-TWO YEARS INTO THEIR LONG MARRIAGE, IN FERNANDINO BEACH, FLORIDA.

because every time I'd go around her house I'd have some food and she loved good food. After my mother died, I didn't have any stability at all. Got a cousin in this town, an aunt in that town, a grandmother all around. I just didn't have any stability as far as family was concerned. I wanted to have that. I made that decision early on. When I get married, I'm going to get me a wife and we're going to have a family.

"This lady, Auretha, impressed me," Jethro continues. "I bought her an engagement ring and put it on her finger. I paid $50.00 for it. It was a diamond ring. That lady done took the ring off her finger and she pawned it to help pay the rent. I was making $9.50 a week. Then Old Man Roosevelt turned the thing around in 1941 and made the NRA, National Recovery Act. It raised our salary to $12.50 a week. She was making $5.00 a week at a hospital. For extra money, she would wash the patients' pajamas. I was doing the same thing. Working twelve hours, from sunup to sundown. We'd pool our money. We rented a house and our rent was due on Saturday, and I didn't have it. Saturday evening the man came by and put a rent card on our apartment. This embarrassed us. People talked about it. The rent wasn't but $16.00 a month. We didn't have it. The house belonged to our pastor's wife and she went down there and scolded the man. She said, 'Don't you ever do that again. These children here are scuffling trying to make it and you're so cheesy for money that you'd do that to a couple that's trying to get started.'"

"He made the money and I was the bookkeeper," Auretha adds.

Jethro beams, "I tell everybody she's the chairman of my finance committee."

"My parents told me," Auretha says, "if you can't pay like you promised, tell the people, whatever it is. If you owe somebody, you don't say nothing, they think you're ignoring it. The next thing you know, they got some kind of warrant against you, because you haven't told them anything."

"We been through so much together," Jethro points out, "that I can look at her and tell something isn't right. Or she can look at me and say, what happened? We communicate. Sometimes she don't feel like talking and will go in the bedroom and shut the door. I'll say, 'Oh, she'll be all right in awhile.' When she says, 'Hey Jeff, bring me some water,' then I know she's okay. She just needed time to get it off her chest. We have more fun sometimes, that you'd think the house was full of folks.

Isn't nobody here but me and her, just communicating. Don't ever go to bed angry. If you don't have peace of mind, you aren't going to rest."

"One time we got to fussing," Auretha recalls, "and I couldn't come to no agreement with him. He wasn't understanding what I was saying and I wasn't understanding what he said. It was a misunderstanding on both parts. I go in there and close the door and go to bed. I'll say my prayers, but I have gone to bed angry and it bothers you all night.

"Whatever we was fussing about that night," Auretha continues, "it feels like it's with me the next morning. I'll say, 'I'm sorry we had the misunderstanding.' Then I'll go about my business and I'm through with it. Whether he was at fault or whether I was at fault. When it's stopped me from sleeping and when I have told you that I'm sorry, whatever the situation, I'm not going back in there and argue about it. That's the end of it."

"What she was talking about is you don't fall out of love," Jethro admits. "You build love. I love that girl better now than I did sixty years ago, six weeks ago, or a week ago. I learned how to love differently all the time, and that's necessary. Knowing how to relate to folks and knowing their ways is important.

"When I wake," Jethro continues, "I kiss her. She likes that. She likes to know that she's at least thought about. Then the day gets started right. If I go out here and don't say nothing that girl's worried all day long. I know that about her. So since I know what she likes, I give it to her. Some-times marriages get to the point where you go to the preacher. We haven't had that yet."

"We haven't ever gone to see the preacher," Auretha adds.

"We come close," Jethro chimes in. "Anybody in their right mind ought to know that there are no two people perfect. You going to mess up and make some mistakes. There's a whole lot out there to get you involved. It could be a serious involvement or a friendly working relationship. I made the mistake of getting involved with someone else, once. I wasn't going to do that anymore. I tell other folks the same thing. I'm not getting involved in that because you trying to mess up my marriage. I am not going to let you do that. No, no, no, no, no, this is the end of the line. You can cry all you want to, but I'm gone now, bye-bye."

"I found out and forgave him," Auretha offers, "Then we talked about it, so that he would know that I knew and what was he going to do about it? If he's going to continue on the same road that he's on, we can't stay together. When you find out, face it, talk about it, and then whichever one that got caught, make a promise—I won't do it no more. You get a feeling when something's going on. There's a difference in the actions. Then after a while it'll come to the surface. You know something is wrong."

"Get it out," Jethro insists. "Get it over with and bring all your cards to the table. Look at this thing. Once it's done, we won't bring that up no more. It isn't easy to hold a marriage together. It takes work and it takes prayer. It's a road that's hard to travel if you don't have God with you."

"The blessed part about this," Auretha explains, "is that we have more or less the same friends. We were reared at Ebenezer and we've always done things together. When we were younger, we went out together. We had mostly the same friends, so there wasn't a problem with him staying off with his men friends and I'm staying off with my girlfriends. We had the same friends. We believe in the Word. Doing unto others as you would have them do unto you. When you got the love you say you have or that I feel in my heart, then I don't have a problem. Wherever he goes, he'll be back. What he's doing while he's there or if he's meeting another woman, it's not my problem. You'll run yourself crazy. If he don't have no more respect for himself than to go out doing all this stuff and if his religion doesn't come together enough for him to be true to the love and the marriage, then it's nothing you can do about it."

"We take the aroma of Christianity," Jethro replies, "because it feels good. We're emotionalized or sensitized when we go to church on Sunday, shouting, carrying on, hollering amen or hallelujah. What about all the other days? You go there to get refreshed and strengthened; when you come out you got something to keep it together until you get back. You're not using it as an illusion, just something to make you feel good. I'm not perfect, but we're working towards perfection. There's no perfect marriage. We work to get all the little kinks out, the little, little stuff that don't belong in there.

"You see, I'm stubborn," Jethro admits, "but not to the point that I can't be corrected. When I do something wrong, Auretha says, 'Do you think that's right?' No, that's not right, but I did it. I reflect on it and know she didn't like that. I'm going to try not to do that any more but here it comes again. She says the same little word, 'Do you think that's right?' Now it's me working on something that isn't right in me. It's me, not her!"

"If he got his mind on something," Auretha agrees, "or the way something ought to be, he don't want to change. He says, 'I told you I'm going to do it like this, and this is what I'm going to do.' So I learned that he's going to do it his way; let him go on and do it. After a while it might work itself around. If he got his head set on the way he's going to do something, don't try to change him, let him alone. Sometimes he'll change things his own self."

"If your partner is not your best friend," Auretha continues, "ya'll not going to make it too far. With your best friend you ought to be able to tell anything and to kind of straighten it out, because when you keep things in you your mind goes all kind of ways. Once it comes out into the open, it's not like you thought it was. I feel like he's my best friend. He has helped me all the time. I've never had to see about my children by myself and do all the rearing alone. He's been my partner and we have learned, we are in this and it's equal. Our chores were equal. I got sense enough to know if he's working two or three jobs, he's not going to come home and wash no dishes and cook. I'm home so I can do that, but it's not my special role. He's a good dishwasher."

"I found out early what my wife likes," Jethro laughs. "She likes a clean kitchen and a clean bathroom. I try to keep both of them clean."

"He's never been sitting down hungry and telling me to fix him something to eat," Auretha insists. "If you're hungry, I'm hungry too. I just got home too, so let's do this thing together."

"It hasn't changed," Jethro continues. "It's still like that."

8

GOOD AND TRUE FRIENDS

RENA AND RUDY ENNIS

Married January 15, 1942, · Philadelphia, Pennsylvania

When Rudy and I were kids," Rena recalls, "we would share things and would take our money to go to the movies. It was thirty-five cents. We would write notes to each other in class. We were just twelve years old and, at that time, a boy just didn't come to your house."

"I would follow her home," Rudy adds.

"And my mom would say, 'Is that boy with you?' I said, 'No ma'am.' I was not going to get a beating, no way!"

"I remember that," says Rudy.

"When we got to be sixteen years old," Rena explains, "he asked my mother could he come around to go to the movies with me. She said, 'all right.' We used to go on picnics. The Baptist churches would take us on picnics and the kids, they would snitch a kiss. He'd say, 'Don't you think we're old enough for nature to take its course?' I'd say, 'I don't know what you're talking about.' He'd say, 'Well get off my bicycle until you find out.' I'd walk all the way home. My sister, I'd always take her with me. And when I wouldn't do what she wanted, she'd come back and tell tales on me.

"One day I came in late," Rena admits, "and my grandmother and my aunt, all of them was there. I was friends to the boys, the girls, everybody. I was determined that I wasn't going to do what my aunt and grandmother thought I was going to do—fill the house with babies. I told them, 'If I have a thousand babies, you never have to take any.' I always had a fresh mouth. In those days, you didn't talk back, and I kept a busted lip."

"I used to tell her to be quiet," Rudy says. "Why don't you just keep quiet?"

"They didn't hit you if you didn't talk back," Rena explains. "You was submissive and that was it. I'm not a submissive person. I have to answer back and I always got an answer waiting for ya.' They beat me up real bad this time. I think they hit me every place but the bottom of my feet, and the only reason they didn't hit me there was because I was standing on them."

"They was cold," Rudy adds.

RENA AND RUDY AT THEIR
FIFTIETH WEDDING ANNIVERSARY
CELEBRATION, IN 1992.

"I bolted out the door and Rudy was right behind me," Rena says. "We went up to Rittenhouse Square. He put snow on my mouth, because it was bleeding. He said, 'When we get out of school this June let's run away. Ask them, but if they say no, let's run away and get married.' We saving our money, had some hid away."

"We was already to buy our furniture," says Rudy. "We went and opened our banks and all we had was a bank full of slugs. Her baby sister had cleaned us out and put slugs in it. We didn't know because the bank, it's still nice and heavy. We thought we had money. My sister, God rest her soul," Rena continues. "We putting money in and she taking it out."

"Then we asked to get married," says Rena. "His grandmother didn't want him to get married and my mother said we were too young to know what we're doing. We were good friends and we loved each other, so we got married in January. By April we had our first real big argument. I said to him, 'How much money do you make?' He said, 'None of your blankety-blank business.' 'Are you talking to me?' He said, 'Yeah, I'm talking to you.'"

"Money didn't bother me," Rudy says. "I was young, both of us eighteen."

"The first thing that came to my mind," Rena admits, "is I better go back home before I get pregnant because if I get pregnant Mama's not going to let me in. She asked, 'What happened?' I said, 'I asked him how much money he made and he told me none of my blankety-blank business.' She said, 'Well, you can go on upstairs and spend the night. Tomorrow morning you going back.

You couldn't wait to get out of here. Now, you go right on back and wash his clothes, clean that house, and you fix his meals. You couldn't wait to get grown.' My mother chased me back the next morning. She said, 'You go up there and you get everything out of that room that belongs to you so you'll have nothing to come for.'"

"My mother told me," continues Rena, "'Let me tell you something. Whatever happens in your house you keep it in your house. Something happen, you move into another room or on the couch until you settle it, but don't take your house business to the street.'

"One time we went in the drugstore," Rena explains, "and this girl says to him, 'Are you going to buy me a Valentine?' I'm sitting at the soda fountain."

"I didn't know her from a can of paint," Rudy chimes in.

"Then we buy this little house in South Philadelphia, and we got a car, a brand-new Ford," Rena says. "This girl told me, 'I saw Rudy at the drive-in movie. He had some girl in there. She looked like Naomi.' He was at the movies, with a girl that lived up the street. I have always lived by this: until you can put your hand on something don't worry, just wait. I considered myself a Catholic, and when God wants you to see something, He'll put it right there in front of you. You don't have to go riding, hunting, and peeping around the corner. Just say your prayers and wait and it'll come to you. I go and tell my mother about it. She said, 'He isn't beating you up and he's paying the bills?' I said, 'Yes, ma'am.' She said, 'Isn't nobody else going to take care of you and that little bad boy.' I went on back home."

"It wasn't an affair, not really," Rudy explains.

"You forgive them, but you can't forget," say Rena. "Forgiveness is not forgetting. I always feel like I forgot those instances, because you be so nice to that person, but after awhile you forget about it. But if that person turns right around and does something to you next year, how can you forget and forgive, when you keep doing the same thing over and over. You're not sorry. You've got to have a sense of forgiveness. When you forgive somebody, you do it unconditionally and not hang it over their head. You have to forgive one another and continue to forgive one another. I had to trust him. I guess it's because of the job he had. Sometimes he'd leave home on Monday and wouldn't come back until Wednesday or Thursday. Like the priest told me: if women are so virtuous, where do men find all these virtuous women to run around with? See, you can't blame it all on the men."

"Sometimes I'd stay all week," Rudy adds.

"He and his friend would go to New York and hunt for a job," she says. "They would leave on Friday and came back on Tuesday. The suit looked like he had slept in it. I didn't say anything. He said, 'There isn't any work in New York. Might as well stayed here.' I'm cleaning out the pockets to go to the cleaners. Here's this Savoy Ballroom ticket. I said, 'Oh, they have jobs in the Savoy Ballroom.'"

"Dizzy Gillespie was there and Johnny Lynch, the Lynch Brothers," Rudy explains. "They blow. Both of them blew trumpets and I knew them. I grew up with them. I love music. I always did love music."

"Then one day, he came in and gave all his money to me," Rena adds. "I threw it all over the floor and said, 'I don't want it, it's your money.' Then my girlfriends said, 'Let's go get a job.' Rudy didn't want me to work, but it was sounding so good."

"She was making $49.10 a week," Rudy beams.

"He thought we were rich," Rena laughs.

"We had money saved all over the place," he continues. "Some people can't handle money. I don't know how to handle it. If I handled it we wouldn't have any. We would crash."

RUDY AND RENA IN
SOUTH PHILADELPHIA, DURING
THE MID-1940S, STAND PROUDLY
NEXT TO RENA'S NEW CAR,
A GIFT FROM RUDY.

"You see, each one of you has to find out what you do best," Rena adds. "Each marriage is different. Even if you don't go to work and you stay home and make your own pies and cook, well, you can save money. If you're truly a homemaker and have been taught to handle money, then you know what to do with it. Everybody has to know where they're coming from. I knew that he loved me enough that he would never hit and beat on me. You're not going to beat me and tell me that you love me because if you love me you don't abuse me. I don't think a woman should suffer in a marriage, just to say you're married—that means nothing. Like I told him one time, 'It's a pleasure to have you but it's not a necessity. I can support myself.' We used to go to dances and things, and he loves to dance and I don't. I'd sit back and look."

"I was playing the saxophone," Rudy laughs, "and this woman walks right up to me and says, 'I just love a man who plays the sax.' Rena was sitting right in front of the stage. She didn't say a word."

"If you challenge a man or woman out in the street like that you embarrass them and they're going to get defensive," explains Rena. "Soon as I hit the door, I said, 'Don't you ever . . .' I have a back room, my boudoir. When I slam that door, I'll go away until we can come to some kind of understanding. I won't talk about it anymore that night because we would have been bawling all the way home."

"She didn't say anything," Rudy insists. "Then at intermission, when they pay the musicians, I came down and gave her my money. She still didn't say anything. When we got home and she's in front of the mirror putting her hair up and I'm getting my bedclothes on, then it happens. But what could I do?"

"In situations like that," Rena points out, "you have to be free and relaxed."

"You have to sweat with the audience," laughs Rudy.

"It has to be like that," Rena continues. "A woman is only as nice as the man she's married to and vice versa. A son is only as nice as the woman that he's married to. Always remember that a son has a mother and you're the wife. You come first, but don't ever force him to choose between the two of you. My mother said, 'You can't serve two masters.' I treat his mother like he treats me. If you don't, then you got hostility. It's like an undertow that's pulling all the time. It's not easy. It's not easy. It has taken us awhile to get here.

"Rudy, he'll run the sweeper," Rena admits.

"I'll do the windows," Rudy chimes in, "I do everything! I'll tell you what happened. We went on strike for ninety-three days. Rena was still working. When she came home, I would clean the house. When Rena came up the steps and through the cellar door at four-thirty or quarter to five her dinner was on the table. I cooked, because I was here. Don't tell me that a woman doesn't do anything. I don't care if she doesn't work. By the time she finished cleaning downstairs she started upstairs. By the time she's finished upstairs then its time to come back down. Then she would wash and iron. One week she gave me about twenty-five dollars. I looked at this money. I threw it all over the floor," Rudy says. "I told her, 'This isn't no money. Don't give me that little bit of money hard as I'm working!'"

"I was saving money," Rena replies. "I took the money we saved from the strike and bought the house we live in now."

"I said, 'You just like a cow,'" Rudy continues. "'Every time I get a full bucket of milk you kick it over.' All of her girlfriends knew that she had bought the house. The first night we stayed in this house and they turned the water on, the water started from the third floor and it was coming down just like Niagara Falls. All her girlfriends were ducking me. Nobody looked at me! Boy! They got a closed-circuit thing. You talk about liberated, they know their stuff."

"We bought it 'as is' from the government," continues Rena. "It didn't bother me, because we're friends. "You've got to be friends because sexual desire doesn't last forever. You've got to be good and true friends. You must have a friendship to go with the love. When a man is young, he'll do anything to make up with you to have sex. When he gets older . . ."

"Can't threaten me," Rudy chimes in. "I can cook, wash, and iron myself. We stay busy."

"And every once in a while we go on vacation by ourselves," says Rena. "He went to Jamaica, because his father's people are from Jamaica. He went and was gone for eight days. This acquaintance of mine went to Jamaica too. She told me, 'I don't know what your husband did; I went to his room three times and he never was in there!' I said, 'He didn't go to Jamaica to stay sitting up in a room waiting for you to come see whether he's going to be there.'"

"Yeah, I knew her and I wasn't going to give her no bone to bring back," Rudy explains. "I told them at the desk if anybody comes looking for me, tell them I'm not here. One time I was sitting by the pool looking right at her. Oh, she got very upset. She came back and told Rena, she couldn't ever find me."

"You must have a life," Rena continues. "You must have your own life and your own friends. You got acquaintances, you got coworkers, and you got very few friends."

"When I was on strike, my buddy called up and said, 'Don't wait until you get hurt to holler. You need anything, let me know,'" Rudy says. "I got about three like that. Rena told one of my buddies one time when he came by, he said, 'Rudy home?' She said, 'No, he didn't get here yet.' He said, 'I'll sit outside.' She said, 'If you can't come in here now, you can't come in here when he gets home.'"

"What he think I'm going to do—attack him or something?" Rena chimes in. "If he can't come in here and sit down, that means that my husband doesn't trust him to come to his house when he's not here."

"Lady comes here one time," says Rudy, "and I had all kinds of women in here: white, green, blue, and black. She couldn't see, but she could hear us laughing and talking and the music was playing. They were all over the place."

"I was at a Society meeting," Rena says. "She told me, 'Oh your husband had a whole house full of women!' I said, 'Now, if you told me he had one in there, then I'd be worried!' She called herself dropping a dime on him. Even children, don't allow your children to tattle to you about the other. Let them know that they can't take a molehill and make a mountain out of it. Sit down and talk, eyeball to eyeball. If you have a problem, move into another room, sleep on the couch until you can settle it. Each time you move out or he moves out, it's no good."

"Yeah, when you're not getting along or you have a little misunderstanding, don't run out," Rudy cautions. "If you put the cat out, there's always somebody around the corner saying, 'Kitty, kitty, come here, kitty, kitty, kitty.'"

9
Evolving Together

SYLVIA AND ROBERT BOZEMAN

Married May 25, 1968 · Camphill, Alabama

During our freshman year at Alabama A&M University in Huntsville, Alabama, we were both math majors," Sylvia begins. "We met in math class. My high school classmate, who was also a freshman, introduced us, because she thought the two of us would like to meet each other. Robert was very intelligent and handsome. These were both attractive qualities. On our first significant outing, Robert escorted me to the debutante ball at the end of our freshman year. That's when we started to develop a close relationship."

"Sylvia was nice looking and had big legs," Robert says. "She was supposed to be a pretty smart person in class work and I was reputed to be very smart, too. We had some of the same classes, so we would compete. In most of our classes we ran neck and neck. Originally, it was more of a competition than a love affair. To go to the debutante ball, I had to invest some money in a tuxedo."

"That was a real commitment," Sylvia chimes in.

"I figured I got to get my money back some kind of way," Robert laughs. "I rented a tuxedo and escorted her to the ball. That summer we started communicating."

"We started dating pretty regularly during our sophomore year," Sylvia recalls. "I went to a summer program at Harvard between my junior and senior year while he worked in Huntsville. That summer gave me a chance to really think about whether or not Robert was the person I wanted to spend my life with. There were people in that program that I had a chance to observe and decide what qualities I wanted in a person. I could compare him with others. There were a lot of things we had in common. We were both brought up in the church. His father was a minister and mine was a deacon. We had strong family ties. The ethical kinds of issues were important. Treating people a certain way was important. He was dependable. He was true to his word. Over the three years we got more involved. By Christmas of our senior year we were engaged."

"The religious background was a big part of my decision," says Robert. "I also compared her to my previous girlfriend who went to A&M. There was a group of us that came from Montgomery. My girlfriend from high school was in this group. She was kind of wild and dated a lot of people,

SYLVIA AND ROBERT ON THEIR

WEDDING DAY, SATURDAY,

MAY 25, 1968, IN CAMPHILL,

ALABAMA. THEY HAD JUST

GRADUATED FROM ALABAMA A&M

UNIVERSITY IN HUNTSVILLE THE

PREVIOUS SUNDAY.

like football players. We broke up our freshman year and I retrieved all of my materials, high school ring and stuff, and said goodbye. My roommate had a girlfriend back home that he eventually married, so we were mild guys, not running all over the place. I was good friends with Sylvia's family, so giving her a ring wasn't a big thing," Robert recalls. "I had made several trips to her house and knew her mother and father very well."

"We graduated on Sunday and married that following Saturday," says Sylvia. "It was a small wedding with a lot of friends from college."

"At the beginning we had small problems in terms of finances," Robert admits. "I'm very meticulous when it comes to keeping records and she's very loose. We worked out a system where I kept my own records and she kept her own records."

"In other words, I had to get a separate checking account," Sylvia laughs.

"Putting our money together didn't work for us," says Robert. "When all the money is in one pot, good records must be kept of who's writing what checks and so forth. Our first falling out was about keeping good records, so we got separate accounts. She tithed; I didn't. She would say, 'The Lord is going to rain down hail on you if you don't pay your money.' She kept that going for a long time. I eventually started tithing."

"We actually do some things together, like investing," Sylvia admits. "We sit down and decide together in what we will invest. We kind of decided that maybe we're going to be here together forever, therefore it's joint.

"During the second year of our marriage, I can remember being very upset. I can't remember what the disagreement was about. I was crying and thought, there's no way this marriage can last beyond three years," Sylvia recalls. "There was some misunderstanding or belief that I thought couldn't be reconciled. It's very hard for two people to come together and make one life. It takes a lot of give and take and adjusting to work on all the issues that we disagree about. We kept working on it until it evolved. We had to decide that the marriage was worth working on and we had to work hard at making it work. One thing that has helped us throughout our entire marriage is deciding that when we disagreed on something and couldn't come to any reconciliation, the person to whom it meant the most would make the decision. Whatever the issue is, it is usually more important to one person than it is to the other."

"I'm a introvert, a loner, and like to meditate," Robert explains. "I can work a crossword puzzle for five hours. It doesn't bother me. Sylvia's an extrovert and likes to have people around. To keep the marriage together all these years, I know when to be introverted and when not to be. Otherwise I'll destroy the marriage. So I give in and try to be sociable. I'm a good dancer, but if given a choice, I'm probably a better bachelor. I've had to develop the skills over time, to be friendly and outgoing. People think that I have the same personality she has. Many times I shut down and don't go and she seems to understand. By being willing to compromise there have been some benefits. Nothing tangible, but I've developed a better character, more tolerance."

"It's probably hereditary. My mother was always into everything," Sylvia admits. "I feel this responsibility to do things that will help black children. I'm involved in a tutorial program, teaching Sunday school and involved with professional organizations, because there are so few black mathematicians. I get caught up in things that I don't really want to do and it's gotten worse. I've gotten better in terms of the house. I'm so meticulous about things. Not only do I try to keep things organized around the house, I want everybody else to be organized too. Over the years I have relaxed a little bit and let others do their own thing. I haven't relaxed on myself but I've relaxed on trying to get Robert to get involved in everything I'm doing. I keep busy all the time and that drives Robert crazy because he wants me to calm down. I get caught up into duty and feeling like it's my responsibility to do all these things."

"I'm very, very laid back," Robert offers. "Over the years, I've learned that some things you hear and respond to and ignore others. It's been challenging trying to keep her business from spilling over on me. I pick and choose the kind of things that I want to do. The things that really irritate me, I let it go, take a walk or take a ride. There are ways of getting around it."

"I have been trying to adjust to his personality," says Sylvia, "but he has changed. We have both evolved. I see myself picking up some of his traits and he has some of mine. We've had challenges all through the marriage. We've had ups and downs. In each situation we decide that we want to continue the marriage, continue working. We regroup. There were many times that we could have divorced."

"We came along at a time when divorce was not an option," Robert insists. "I'm from a two-parent household, she's from a two-parent household. We were not brought up in an atmosphere where people got divorced. The expectation was that you were going to be together. There's nothing special about being married thirty years to the circle of friends that we belong to. That's the expected thing. When you run into challenges, then you're not looking to divorce. You're trying to figure out how you're going to work this thing out.

"We were married three years when our daughter was born and two years later our son," Robert continues. "Both of us were professionals, and it meant a lot of travel. We agreed that I was going to travel and she'd stay home. When the tables turned that was tough. I had to give up the whole business of the wife staying at home and taking care of the kids. I had to give that up because she wanted to work. She had to go to conventions because that was part of her work. I had to adjust to the additional responsibility for picking up the kids from day care, and taking them here and there. With some of my comrades, the wife did the running around and fetching the kids in addition to working. I wasn't quite that selfish. It didn't happen all at once; I eased into it. Eventually I got used to it. Either I was going to stay there with the two babies or I was going to break up the marriage, and breaking up the marriage was not an option for me. I had to change my attitude toward family, women, and work. Things got more equal."

"I think it's been very hard on men to make that adjustment because what they look for in their wives is what they saw in their mothers, and it's not the same," Sylvia explains. "That has been a big adjustment for all the men who are coming along during this period. Men don't realize what they're going through. They think something is wrong because their wives are not acting like their mothers. They need to communicate about that. Traditional roles are evolving. Women are also having a difficult time trying to balance family and work. There are no role models for the evolution that is taking place. Men need to work together with women to figure out these new roles. They both need to understand that it's something they're going through that everybody else is going through too. It's not peculiar to them."

"Because we're living in changing times, couples must be flexible with how the marriage will progress," Robert explains. "Couples must be willing to make some changes as the marriage goes along and have love, faith, and confidence in their mate. You can't be set in your ways either. I had to make some major adjustments to make our marriage work."

"When we started off we both went to graduate school together," Sylvia continues. "That set a certain expectation. We were both serious about our careers. Once we had kids, I dropped out and took care of them while he finished and went on and got a job. Then I returned to the workforce. It was his turn to take on some of these responsibilities so that I could finish my degree. Turnabout is fair play."

"Religion has played an important part in our marriage too. 'The family that prays together stays together,' that's true," Sylvia insists. "Having a spiritual base sustains me through difficult times. My faith and relationship with God sustain me. When things are very difficult I have faith that it will work out. As I continue to go through difficulty and rely on my faith, it strengthens me. When I need someone to talk with I call my girlfriends. I've had girlfriends who would sit up late at night and help me turn the situation over and look at the problem from different angles. Not give advice, because I don't need advice. I just want someone to help me look at the problem from different sides and then I figure out what I want to do. I talk with male friends too."

"Religion was more important during our dating years," Robert offers. "We were on the same page when it came to religion, values, beliefs, and church. That helped us with the relationship. It would be very difficult for one believer to be married to a nonbeliever and then raise a family. I can't see how that's done."

"Normally, communication comes from Sylvia to me," Robert continues. "Most of the time she will tell me what she wants me to know, what I need to know, and what I need to do. I say, 'Okay.'"

"I consult with him on various things without assuming that he's going to go along with it," Sylvia explains. "We use sensitivity. The other person has concerns, feelings, and a schedule, so we take that into consideration. Telling someone what to do assumes that you have authority over the other person. Consulting indicates more equality and a mutual consideration. We consult."

"It has to be that way when you have two people involved with two different schedules," Robert agrees. "There's not a lot of spontaneous stuff going on. Most of it's predictable and planned. When we're going to go out to a play, we usually get tickets. We did a lot of spontaneous stuff when we were young. Predictability is important to me now."

"We go out to dinner once a week on Friday nights," says Sylvia. "We have common activities and concerns. We call each other at work during the day, not every day. I call just to let him know that somebody's thinking about him."

"It makes me feel loved to know that we have general concern for each other," Robert admits.

"He is concerned and understanding when I'm doing all this late working and doesn't have a fit about it," adds Sylvia. "To rejuvenate our marriage we go away together. Several times a year we go away, some planned, some spontaneous. We'll get in the car, ride, and decide what direction we want to go. There are low periods in every marriage when you don't feel romantic love. During those times you need to be married to a friend, because you can co-exist until the romantic love returns. Robert is my friend."

"And Sylvia is my friend," Robert beams.

10

We Are in This until the End

BRENDA AND AARON TURPEAU

Married April 19, 1964 · Covington, Kentucky

Aaron had a girlfriend, but he was also interested in my roommate," Brenda begins. "He was real cute. I was interested in another guy at the time and Aaron was supposed to be my go-between with this other guy. In the meantime with all this communication and hanging around him, I begin to like him. I never took him seriously because I knew about his escapades and I also had a boyfriend back home."

"When she came to West Virginia State College as a freshman, I was a big-time sophomore," says Aaron. "Somehow I got the message from one of her friends that she kind of liked me. I was going to break up with my girlfriend, but I wasn't ready to settle down. In October of that year, I started pledging Alpha Phi Alpha and couldn't talk to girls while I was on line. One of my big brothers suggested that I see her in the back of the student union, where nobody could see us. We arranged to meet. I told her that evening that I was not interested in a girlfriend at the time, but I'd like to marry her one day. I didn't want a girlfriend because I had some things I wanted to do. I went to kiss her on her forehead, then she kissed me!"

"He always says that," Brenda laughs.

"During my junior year we became an item on campus," says Aaron. "This was a small campus, only about 600 kids on a black campus. When she went home for Christmas, I got the word as soon as we got back to school that Brenda went home to be engaged to this longtime boyfriend. I was shocked. I had invested a year and a half. No sooner than I had heard about it that I went to her dormitory and said I needed to talk."

"I didn't take Aaron seriously," exclaims Brenda.

"She told me about this guy, and said they weren't engaged," says Aaron.

"But it was serious," Brenda admits.

"I said, 'Let's talk about this right now,'" Aaron says. "All she's got to do is tell me, because I put everything out there. She said that she didn't know. I said, 'Until you make up your mind, we got to split.' So we split up and the word went all around campus. By the time I got to the frat room, a half hour later, my boys already knew and I was ridiculed. I was convinced it was going to have to be her move if we were to get together. She had to decide."

"Ego!" Brenda chimes in. "At the time I was confused. Sometimes I loved him more, and sometimes I loved the other person more. I could not figure it out. You have to keep in mind that I did not take him seriously because the feedback came to me about what he was doing. We used to call it 'creeping.' He was creeping. I was on line and my sorority sisters heard about it, in detail. I was surprised, but I did understand, because I couldn't give him an answer. I couldn't lie because this was serious business."

"One thing that was important to me in this process," Aaron recalls, "was that she came to me one day in the cafeteria, after about a week, and asked if we could be friends."

"He wasn't speaking," Brenda insists. "We'd pass each other on campus and he wouldn't say good morning. He was mad!"

"I wasn't mad," Aaron replies. " I treated her like I did everybody else. I didn't want to be her friend. My ego was crushed! I had to put on a front and not speak—be cool—but I was crushed. Then I got the word from one of my fraternity brothers that she wanted to come back."

"Everybody was trying to get us back together," Brenda recalls. "His friend Sam said, 'I'm going to make an arrangement for you and Turpeau to meet and talk.' I said he wouldn't even speak to me. He said, 'I'll arrange for you to call him at eight o'clock and I'll have him by the telephone. Are you going to call?' I said, 'Yeah.' He said, 'You want to get back together?' I said, 'Yeah, it would be nice to get back together, because he's a really nice guy.' He set up the arrangement and I called. Sam answered the phone and he said, 'I'm going to go get Turpeau.' I later learned that Turpeau was standing right there! Then we started talking."

"That was a very important conversation," says Aaron. "I said, 'What would you like to do?' She had to commit. She had to come out and say that she wanted to see me—that she wanted to get back together. She said she wanted to get back together. I said okay, we can talk about it. I ran across campus so fast! I was on the other side of campus in two minutes."

"I had been thinking during the three-week period about our breakup," Brenda offers. "When I met a guy, I was thinking about marriage. People got married early. It wasn't that you dated this person and dated that person. I had a lot of serious thinking to do. I had my pen and pad and weighed the pros and cons of the different guys, and Aaron came out on top in just about everything."

"We talked and then we laid out the plan of how she was going to dump this dude."

"Yeah, he helped me dump him," Brenda exclaims.

"She wrote the letter to this guy. I reviewed the letter, and we went to the mailbox together to mail this letter!" Aaron says.

"Aaron was dependable," Brenda offers. "He was warm and friendly. He had a

 AARON AND BRENDA ON THEIR FIRST DATE AT THE WEST VIRGINIA STATE COLLEGE STUDENT UNION, OCTOBER 1961.

lot of potential. I invited him to my home in Hopkins, South Carolina. I grew up on a farm. He's the first guy that my dad liked. My dad said that Aaron appeared to be a real gentleman."

"Brenda was very pretty and still is," Aaron points out. "I'd had a few girlfriends before, but I was never serious about anybody to the extent of having a long-term relationship. She was the first one I wanted to put on a pedestal. She had a lot of good qualities. That's why I told her that I could not date her because I had some fooling around to do. I wanted to party some more. This is my jewel. It wasn't because we had a lot of conversation. I just knew it.

THE TURPEAU FAMILY

AROUND 1973: AARON, BRENDA,

AARON JR., AND MICHEL.

"At the end of my junior year and her sophomore year, I gave her my pin," Aaron continues. "When you pinned someone that was just like an engagement. People on campus couldn't believe it. She was transferring, so I pinned her. That was a big thing for us. In other words, I'm saying, 'Here is my commitment.'"

"I transferred to Mt. Mercy College in Pittsburgh, Pennsylvania," Brenda says, "because I wanted to get a certain course of study and they didn't have it at West Virginia State."

"She was away and we were in love. She would come back and visit me on campus."

"He got caught one of those times too," Brenda chimes in. "I said, Turpeau, you are doing it again!"

"We married the last April of my senior year," Aaron continues. "It was time to settle down, so we decided to get married. I graduated in May and she came back down to the graduation. Brenda visited Cincinnati and met my family and they liked her. They had seen a couple of the other girls before, but they really liked her. She was well received by my family and by friends of my family."

"I had promised my father that if I got married I would finish school," Brenda recalls.

It was important for us in the South, and our parents had always taught us that we needed an education. He said, 'If you get married you have to promise me that you'll finish school.' I made that promise."

"When we got married my father offered us a wedding or money," says Brenda. "He said the practical thing is to take the money. We took the money. I didn't regret not having a wedding, because very few couples in those days had weddings. My youngest sister had a wedding so that was 'our' wedding."

"Right after we got married, Brenda got pregnant. She came and lived in Cincinnati, my hometown, while I taught school. After that year of teaching school, we went to Pittsburgh for her to finish school."

"Having to be responsible for somebody other than yourself was difficult," Brenda recalls. "I went to school full-time and we had a baby. I had to manage a home, had to pay bills, and had to cook everyday. Being responsible was a big adjustment. Sometimes I got angry."

"She couldn't get any help from me," admits Aaron.

"He's that old-fashioned kind," Brenda explains.

"They call it chauvinistic," Aaron smiles.

"Yeah, chauvinistic," Brenda continues. "In the evenings after work he would come home and sit down. I'd get angry. How come both of us are out there working and both of us are busy. He gets to come home and sit down, read the paper, and I have to go straight to the kitchen. I don't even get to take my clothes off.

"When I was about seven months pregnant with my second child, we were living in Cincinnati in our first little home. We both worked full-time. He left teaching school at about three o'clock and went to his mother's house each day to take a nap. Then he'd come pick me up at five-thirty from Jewish Hospital, where I worked as a medical records administrator. We would then go by and pick up the baby from the nursery. We came home and, on this particular day, Aaron laid on the sofa and I went to the kitchen. About ten minutes later, he yelled into the kitchen, 'When will dinner be ready?' I exploded."

"I didn't understand the pressure that she was under," Aaron offers. "I would go by my mom's and dad's house and be very comfortable while she was going to pieces. Since it was my hometown I had escapes. She was in a strange town; therefore, the adjustment was much harder for her. I was very comfortable going by my parents' house and cooling out. I was immature because, when we first got married, I still wanted to hang with the boys at the frat house. I don't think it lasted too long. I eventually grew up."

"When I was pregnant, it seemed like he was out every night at the fraternity house. I told him, 'Aaron, if this baby happens to come one night while you're out, you can forget it, because I'm taking my baby home to South Carolina and don't come looking for us.' One night close to my due date, he was out and I said, 'I'm going to fix him tonight.' I heard him coming up the stairs to the apartment. I jumped out of bed, made it up, and got in the shower and pulled the curtain. He came in and turned on the light. He was quiet. He looked around and said, 'Oh my God, I did it now!' He ran through the living room, fell over a chair, and, as he reached for the doorknob, I said 'Aaron, where are you going?'"

"I melted on the door," Aaron states. "I was scared out of my wits."

"He straightened up a little bit after that. It's in his blood, he inherited it."

"I was the one in charge of everything during this time in our lives," continues Brenda. "I felt like I had to take care of everything, the bills, baby, and work. I felt like I had to do it, for it to get done."

"My mother paid the bills and stuff in our house," Aaron admits. "I grew up in a household where my mother taught school and she was in charge of paying the bills. My concept was, here's the money, do whatever you want."

"Initially, that was tough," Brenda explains. "The first couple of years were rough years financially. There wasn't much money to go around."

"I was taught to be the provider and to be socially conscious," says Aaron.

"Bourgeois," Brenda chimes in. "He grew up in an upper-middle-class family. My family was a little bit different. My father was the head of the house. My mother never worked outside of the home, and my father took care of everything. I came from a loving family with strong Southern

Baptist ethics and morals. My father was a farmer and a lumberman. My people were entrepreneurs and they worked very hard. My father was a cotton farmer and my mother worked in the fields. The men were heads of the house. I came into the marriage expecting to be taken care of, provided for. My mother was submissive, but I have never been submissive.

"I was young and in a strange town," Brenda continues. "This was a super-conservative town, and Aaron led me to believe we were in the North. I was really surprised."

"It was really 'up South,' and that wasn't saying very much," Aaron admits. "There were few things going on. The South was much more active."

"I had a rough time during the first few years of our marriage," Brenda recalls. "Aaron would tell me that he was going to be somewhere on time and he never was there. He's always running behind. It has been thirty-five years and I haven't gotten over that. And the other thing is, he doesn't pick up his clothes. My mother said, 'I'll tell you what, he's a pretty good guy. He works, he doesn't run the street, and he takes care of you—kick the clothes under the bed.' My mother gave me some good advice."

"She gets bossy: she's opinionated and hard-headed. She feels she has good reason to be and it's difficult for her to compromise. I ignore it very well," Aaron admits. "I walk away when she gets opinionated."

"It's because he doesn't listen and he won't talk. Those are the things in our marriage that we've really had to work on," Brenda explains. "He's not a communicator. At first, he didn't communicate at all. I had to read his mind. I didn't know what he was thinking. I kept talking and sometimes I'll say you are not going to budge until you hear me. He's learned to listen as the years have gone by."

"I won't respond because it may cause conflict," Aaron cautions. "I think we can work through it without the conflict, but when there's conflict we don't listen to each other. Most people call it conflict; I call it difference of opinion. We've never had a conflict over money, since I've never had the checkbook. I make the money and she spends the money. Spending money correctly is hard. Doing correct spending so we prosper is hard. All of my friends make more money than I make and always have. Brenda can manage money. She knows how to handle money because of her family's background. Therefore we live decently. I don't worry and I've never worried. She gets mad with me and says, 'Why don't you do this?' She gets tired.

"One of the keys to this relationship was when it dawned on me what makes me happy," Aaron says. "It was one of the few times I've wept in our relationship. I realized that what makes me happy is for her to be happy. I understand that."

"Aaron and I made a commitment to each other to make this marriage work in the very beginning. We said, we're in this together. I respect him and he respects me. We decided that come hell or high water we are in this until the end."

"I told her even when we get a divorce we're going to live together! I can't imagine life without Brenda. I just can't get through life without her."

"I'm glad I chose him that day in the dormitory at West Virginia State. I made a good choice, a very good choice. I don't regret that choice at all."

"I'm just so happy," Aaron replies. "It's nothing easy; you must work at it."

11

Respect Each Other as Individuals

PATRICIA AND GEOFFREY HEARD

Married April 2, 1966 · Atlanta, Georgia

I was working at Washington High School," Pat begins. "A mutual friend said that she knew a young man near her hometown that she wanted me to meet. I told her that I had met enough people and was not interested in meeting anybody else. She and her husband were having a party and invited us so that we would meet."

"It was a little better than a blind date, because there were so many others to talk with at the party," says Geof. "I had refused to go on any more blind dates."

"Geof was very pleasant. Everybody was talking and joking. There was nothing of any real significance that came between us at that party, but we exchanged phone numbers."

"I met somebody else that evening, though I did talk with Pat," Geof admits.

"He did the follow-up calling," Pat says. "I'd never been accustomed to calling, being the initiator. We talked about our backgrounds, mutual interests, and our jobs. We were getting acquainted."

"Initially, I was partly being kind," says Geoffrey. "Our friends were nice enough to introduce us, so I was being kind to follow through by calling Pat. After a while I began to feel that maybe this was somebody I ought to pursue or get to know better. After all, I wasn't getting any younger. Our conversations encouraged the follow-up. She seemed like a nice person, intelligent and not just out there to pursue men. I was tired of being pursued. I don't say that to flatter myself, but I was getting tired and she was not one to pursue me. She let it happen, which I appreciated."

"When my friend told me about Geof, she said, 'He's a little wild. He needs someone to help tame him and I believe you could do it,'" says Pat. "He was a little cocky, but not in the way that some fellas are. He was proud and had pride in his school, Morehouse College. After six months of meeting him, we decided to date regularly. When we first met he was traveling a lot."

"I worked for a beauty supply company, covering six states doing beauty shows promoting the product," says Geof.

"With all female clients," Pat smiles.

"During the six-month period, Pat did something that I thought was really bold. She, our friends, and my sister planned a surprise birthday party for me. I had been out of town and it was never a certainty when I was going to get back. That was one of the few times that anyone has ever planned a surprise birthday party for me. If she's bold enough to try to pull it off, she's got a lot of nerve. I got back in town in the mid-afternoon and my friend took me out for drinks to keep me busy. He kept me busy and I had no idea. They pulled it off, and it worked. I was impressed, and our relationship began going uphill. We dated for almost two years and then began talking about getting married. The only time her parents commented about us was when we sat down and told them we were getting married."

"We were asking for their blessing," Pat says. "They wanted to know about his background, his family, his sister. My mother may have had more to say than my father about Geof. Oftentimes we would go to the couple's house that introduced us. Geof is an avid card player. He would get in a card game; invariably, one hand led to another. One more, one more, one more, and sometimes it would get a little late. My mother didn't like that I was getting home late. She would fuss. She said, 'He shouldn't bring you home this late. The next time he comes here to pick you up, I'm going to tell him not to bring you home late like this again.' She never said a word to him, just to me. He's there enjoying himself and I'm thinking about what a hard time I'll have once I get home. I never said anything. I was too embarrassed to say anything about it even though I was working at my first job. I was grown, but I didn't want to say that I had to be at home at a certain time. My mom wanted me home at midnight. We wouldn't leave until about one or two. If we went out to a dance, we would have breakfast, then it wouldn't be until about two-thirty or three."

"My mother was always complimentary of Pat," Geof recalls. "The only thing she said was, 'That girl is just too clean, she's going to wipe herself to death.' My parents were happy that I was getting married. They were old fashioned. When you're out there too long, they figured that you are going to get in trouble and get tied up with the wrong folks. My sister and Pat were friends, so they checked her out through my sister."

"They probably knew a lot more than I realized," replies Pat. "So many people said that Geof tried to pick a wife like his sister. His sister Helen and I are so much alike in our thinking and acting."

"Some people say she favors my sister," Geof admits.

"Geof's father died the second year of our marriage. The more I hear about him the more I wish I had known him better. He was a real visionary," Pat recalls. "He could calculate, write well, a real smart man with such deep beliefs, with no formal education."

"One time Pat's mother and I had a little confrontation," Geof offers. "She wanted her daughter to do something, I can't remember what, but when we finished cursing each other out she was woman enough to say, 'We're through with that.' We both got what we had to say off our chests and then we apologized."

"My mother's biggest problem was she didn't want me to get married. It wouldn't have mattered to whom. She just couldn't get over the fact that I was now married," Pat points out.

"She was a little bit possessive, bossy, and aggressive," Geof replies. "She would run your life if you allowed her, but I wasn't the one. She was smart, but she learned that that wasn't going to work with me."

GEOFFREY AND PATRICIA
ON THEIR WEDDING
DAY, APRIL 2, 1966,
IN ATLANTA, GEORGIA.

"After we married, I didn't go by the house to see her every day. She probably thought that Geof was taking me away from her," says Pat. "Before marrying, I was working and sharing my earnings liberally with my family, doing things around the house and making things comfortable for them. It was kind of rough for her to give that up."

"I had to let her know that this was my house," Geof states adamantly. "She runs that house over there, but she isn't going to run this one. When we cleared the air, she respected me until the day she died and I respected her. We were the best of friends.

"When dating, one of the things that made me have feelings for Pat was that she respected what I was doing," explains Geof. "She was never on me about changing my habits, like the card playing. She doesn't play cards, but she respected the fact that I like to do this. That's what attracted us and that's what continues to keep us together. Each of us has a head of our own. I never tried to change her and she never tried to change me; we respect each other as individuals."

"I agree with that wholeheartedly," says Pat. "Develop your own interests, your own hobbies. Don't try to become one immediately; you'll grow to become one. Somewhere down the line you will need to be your own person.

"The thing that really made me fond of Geof more than other men was his promptness and keeping his word. If he said that he was going to pick me up, he was on time. He never called to cancel or to change plans. I could count on him. Many times I wouldn't be ready because I'm a little slow, but he would be there before time. It's pretty much the same to this day. He has not disappointed me, only with the little things I want him to do around the house. What also impressed me was his fondness for nice things and going nice places. I got a chance to get around to some very lovely eating places, with candlelight meals. He was not cheap. He sort of swept me off my feet. He would always have something in mind or always had an idea about where we were going or what we should do. For some people that may be a problem, but it was never a problem with me because of the way he handled it. He would ask, 'What do you think about such and such a thing?' Other guys were cheap. Geof was very generous. What really carried him over the top was his generosity with my sister. I have a younger sister, ten years younger. She got a chance to go with us and that was not a problem for him. Geof included her a couple of times. With others, she got cast aside."

"I'm the youngest of twelve children," says Geof. "Therefore I got a chance to learn a lot from my siblings' mistakes. My mother was forty-seven and my dad was fifty when I was born. There are almost thirty years between my oldest sister and me. I had a very firm dad. My mama was more lackadaisical. She didn't push much. Dad was a very stern disciplinarian. They supported all of us to the best of their ability and encouraged us to do the right thing. That's where I got my character."

"My mother was the strong disciplinarian and my dad was lackadaisical and very forgiving," says Pat. "Like his parents, they were interested in our getting an education. They were good parents. We grew up in a public housing project. At that time, the housing projects were good places to live. Many of my friends had a mother and father in the home, and their whole goal was to save enough money to move out and buy a home. Though they didn't have formal training, they had aspirations. We moved out when I was in the sixth or seventh grade."

"Before we married, I was Methodist and Pat was Baptist," Geof recalls. "We talked about our religions before we got married, decided together that we would join the Presbyterian Church, and the minister there married us. We believe there's only one God. People have different methods of worshiping. We pray pretty regularly. It's not ritualistic. When we married, God put a blessing on our marriage. We would not have been as fortunate without His blessing. I'm not one of those Christians who believes that every word I have to say is bless you, Jesus, and thank you, Jesus. You serve God by doing. God called us to be doers and not talkers. Doing is also important in a marriage, not just talking."

"And most of the times, it's not inside the church building," Pat chimes in. "It's what you do after you leave."

"My patience is short with those talking Christians," Geof continues. "One of the things my mentor,

THE HEARD FAMILY
IN OCTOBER, 1979:
GEOFFREY, PATRICIA, AND THEIR
DAUGHTER, JENNIFER.

Dr. Benjamin Mays, impressed upon me was, 'When you leave here, you want to live and do something where something or somebody will be better because you came this way.' That's my philosophy too. If there's a homeless person who is going through something, help them. If there is a child out there who needs help, do that. And do it without fanfare. Do it because it needs to be done.

"Though we had similar values, we had conflict from time to time," Geof points out. "This wouldn't be a biggie with some people but it was with Pat. The fall of the first year we were married, we went to homecoming. Several of the fellas came back by the house and were a little bit inebriated. She told me, 'I don't like it and don't do that any more.'"

"I said, there are plenty of hotel rooms in the city," Pat chimes in.

"I understood," Geof admits. "She doesn't drink and doesn't like that, so why push it. There was a time when she wanted to jump on me about something during that first year. All I did was push her in the closet and hold the door shut. She was much smaller and weighed about ninety-five pounds. I held the door until she asked me to let her out. I said, if you cool down. Obviously, we've had arguments. We've had differences. We've had plenty of them. My dad taught me to do this. He said, 'One person can't argue with themselves.' When she gets upset the worst thing I can do is get the newspaper and start reading. If you decide that you're not going to agree, why keep arguing about it? I say, that's your opinion, that fine, I'm through with it. Then go on reading the paper. She might be mad a couple of days, but she'll be all right."

"He tends to forget it, and I'll continue to think about it long afterwards," Pat replies. "Three or four days down the road I may mention something else about it. I probably don't get things off my chest right away. I have this inner feeling that I want to say something, but I don't know how to say it right then. Two or three days later, I figure out how I should have said it. That tends to be the way I react to most things. I tend to weigh everything too heavily and think too long before expressing myself. There have been instances or issues that are not a part of the marriage that I regret that I didn't speak up. It's sort of like the sin of omission. Maybe that one little voice could have made a difference. They say opposites attract; it's true, we're opposites. That's what I like about him. Geof speaks right up right away. I wish that I could do that. I'm attracted to that."

"She sits back, lets me worry and have the headaches," Geof chimes in. "She enjoys it. She'll live a long time. That's why women live longer than men."

"At one time my hobby was sewing. Every other evening I was in some fabric store buying fabric and patterns. I was a 'fabric-holic,' just like an alcoholic, spending heavily on fabric and sewing accessories. Geof spoke to me several times about all of the checks written to fabric stores. He said, 'You must open up another bank account.'"

"When she wrote a couple of bounced checks, that stopped her from spending so much on fabric," Geof insists. "It really gave her a sense of how it works. When we were putting our money together she didn't have a sense of what she was really spending, so it appeared as if she didn't care.

"In the seventies I started my own company with a partner," Geof continues. "We couldn't have gone into business at a worse time, because that was when the market was tight. Everything went wrong, but we survived. We made loans and did what we had to do. If you know that you have no money, what is there to be frustrated about? We never had a whole lot."

"I wasn't too happy about it," says Pat. "Geof kept saying that it was going to work. What was comforting was, he said, 'Don't worry because as long as the Lord keeps me healthy and strong we're going to have somewhere to live and something to eat.' It was comforting to know that he was going to do everything he could to make a living for us. He wanted to start the business, so why stop him? We've always had freedom and flexibility in our marriage. He's encouraged me to pursue my interests. It was only after we married that I finished my Master's with his help and cooperation. There are times when he gets away with the boys and I with my social club or sorority. I haven't ever felt tied down and bound."

"We let each other have space," Geof insists. "That's what makes it. I don't cramp her style and she doesn't cramp mine. When we allow the other to be themselves, we're happy. If you cramp somebody else you going to get cramped. We started that from day one. With all the space we allow each other, infidelity has not been an issue. I've learned from others and have seen friends who had that experience and went separate ways. Other friends who were in that situation forgave and forgot. Don't ever say what you won't do because you don't know. Fortunately, we have not had to cross that bridge."

"I'm glad that we haven't had that problem," Pat adds. "It's not even been a wish on my part. I couldn't deal with that. I can't divide myself in another relationship like that. When we hear things like that on television and from friends, I always tell Geof, 'Ooh, that wouldn't be me! You would have to go!' I think women know sometimes and don't say anything because they would have to take action. I have even asked him sometimes, 'Have you been unfaithful?'"

"I tell her, 'Have you caught me? If you haven't caught me I've been faithful,'" Geof laughs.

"You never know what you will actually do, but I put too much faith and confidence in making our marriage work. And then for him to mistreat me that way, I could never get over it. Often Geof tells me that I need to start going to the grocery store with him. He says it gets hot in there sometimes."

"Women flirt; they're aggressive," Geof smiles. "It's fun to me. They say, 'Who are you cooking for? You can bring that over to my house and we'll have dinner.' A whole lot of women don't want a single man. The young girls definitely don't. I tell them, I got a lady that gets everything I got and she's going to get everything when I'm gone. Older guys, especially older men, get so stupid and weak and go for the young ones. One lady told me, 'I don't have to wash no drawers or no socks. I take him, use him, and send him home to his wife.'"

"I'm a gregarious person," admits Geof, "and I'm involved with lots of people and projects. She gets a little bit upset because I don't know how to say 'no.' That could have been a problem without a more understanding and respecting person, especially when others say 'I must get home.' I never had a curfew."

"It makes me tired to hear all the things he has to do," Pat says. "I don't sit around thinking about it—I'm too involved with other things. When I have other things on my mind, I don't have evil thoughts because I'm occupied. I have a life too."

"I am also nontraditional," Geof admits. "I make no bones about the fact that I cook. A lot of guys say, 'Oh you must be henpecked,' as far as I'm concerned. Far from it. There are a lot of other things that I do that would probably make others think that Pat is domineering. If you don't fit the typical traditional roles of husband and wife, that means you're henpecked, particularly for men. I'm not going to fit into the traditional mold.

"If somebody had told me in 1966 that I'd be married this long I would have told them they're crazy!" Geof smiles. "It's been surprising for me. I prayed, I hoped, and I wanted it to work."

"Geof makes me feel secure. Not as far as material things, but with who he is and his character. His strong personality makes me feel good. I really appreciate this emotional security," admits Pat.

"Everybody needs somebody. When the chips are down, Pat is there for me. I've got a partner in this. Whatever happens, my partner's going to be there. The challenges out there are difficult enough, but when I finish I can go home. Even if I lose the battle out there, I can retreat to home," Geof smiles.

12
BLIND DATE

PAULINE AND CHARLES COFFEY

Married June 29, 1957 · Charlotte, North Carolina

It was a blind date," recalls Pauline. "My friend's husband, who was a friend of Charles, introduced us. They were coming home from the army and she said 'I got somebody I want you meet.' They set up the date. I was a little bit excited because I had never been on a blind date before. Dinner went well, and afterwards we went to a drive-in movie. Then it started blooming."

"You forgot to tell her what a nice fella they told you I was," Charles laughs.

"I don't know if it was quite those words!" Pauline smiles affectionately.

"I was home on furlough and I didn't have anything thing to do. My friend, Clemmy Watson, asked me if I wanted to meet a desperate young lady," Charles laughs. "I had never been on a blind date and I guess I was concerned about what kind of girl she would be. Clemmy was a very conservative fellow, and I was conservative, too. I guess that's why we were friends. I was a little apprehensive of who I was going to meet, but when I saw her, I said 'she's okay' and we started talking."

"Charles made his decision to pursue me at first sight," Pauline says. "During that time, it was so different from dating now. When you went out, your parents had a special time for you to be back. I can appreciate that. It was a time when you knew you had to be a lady and respectable. You would not date anybody that you would think was not going to respect you. Knowing that he was from the lifestyle, almost, that I was, made it a little easier."

"We dated several times before I went back to Colorado," Charles says.

"It was about two weeks and then he had to go back."

"I told her I'd write," Charles continues, "and she said, 'I'll write you' and we did."

"I guess at that time, I just kind of figured that was about it," Pauline explains. "I knew that I would write him if he would write me, which he did."

"But were you interested in me?" Charles chimes in.

"I must admit I was," Pauline replies. "Being a service guy, he traveled around to different places and met lots of people. He was really a nice guy and had been that way for most of the time we were together. He was kind of like my father, nice, even-tempered, yet fun. I think that helped a lot."

"I wrote first, but she was standing by the mailbox every day to see if I had written her," Charles laughs.

"We wrote back and forth pretty often," Pauline recalls.

"She got bold one time. She told me when I got discharged not to pick up anybody along the way. Coming home, I was driving alone, and she says, 'Look, if you want me to, I'll come out and drive back with you.'"

"I did not!" Pauline exclaims.

"We dated for about two years. After I proposed, we married in about six months. I'd searched around for a ring," Charles explains. "Then one day while I was working at the post office I saw the ring that I could afford in a catalog. I purchased it. When I gave it to her we were home alone. We talked and talked and I was getting ready to leave. I just pulled out the ring and asked her if she would accept it. She grabbed it!"

"No, I did not," Pauline explains. "I said I had to think about it. I had to think about it because, after all, I was my father's oldest daughter and he was not ready to let me go, even at that age. Of course, I wasn't living at home, but I would go home on the weekends and I had to give it some thought."

"While I was working at the post office I let her drive my car. I told her to pick me up. She took my car and didn't come back. I was standing out waiting for her to pick me up, and she was driving around joyriding with my car and I had to walk home! Once we got engaged she just took over my car. It wasn't mine anymore. That's right, she started taking control!"

"We were both twenty-seven," Pauline says. "My father met Charles and thought he would be okay for me. He said 'He seems like a nice fellow.'"

"Soon after we married, I continued working at the post office on the night shift," Charles recalls. "The first week that I had gone back to work, I forgot I was married and went home to my parents' house! When I walked in, my mother said, 'What's the matter, you had an argument already?' Then it dawned on me that I was married. She laughed and I went home. What I realized then is that when I got married I had some responsibilities that I couldn't neglect. Before marriage you could do something if you wanted to and delay some of your responsibilities. But I knew then

PAULINE AND CHARLES,

BOTH AGE TWENTY-SEVEN, AT

THEIR WEDDING RECEPTION,

JUNE 29, 1957.

PAULINE AND CHARLES, BOTH AGE TWENTY-SEVEN, AT THEIR WEDDING RECEPTION, JUNE 29, 1957.

that I had a responsibility to my family. Whatever my family did or failed to do, I was responsible and I accepted that responsibility. I've tried to adhere to that message throughout our marriage."

"I knew it was a serious thing," Pauline admits, "but for the first few months, I was scared a little bit because I had never been in this situation before. After a few months I started feeling very relaxed. Of course, I knew my responsibilities and I tried to do what I knew was right. Somehow, I don't know how it happened, but it seems that I was fortunate enough to meet someone that felt the way that I did about life and was a home person too. I wasn't ever one to be away from home a lot and do a lot of running around while I was single. It seems that he was that way, so that really just made it a little smoother for both of us."

"Another thing that helped us," Charles explains. "The experts have told us incessantly that two things cause problems in a marriage. One is infidelity and the other one is finances. With infidelity, I've applied the Golden Rule that my mother told me—treat everyone as you want to be respected. When I'm out, I think, 'How she would feel if she knew I did that? Would she be happy?' Or if she did it, how would I feel? I thought, I wouldn't like it if she did it, then I wouldn't do it, either. And with the finances, from day one it was never my money and your money. We put them together. We save some, take care of our responsibilities, and we take an allowance. We don't argue about money. I don't ever remember arguing about money or anything like that."

"Because we don't have any," Pauline replies.

"I try to interject humor into our marriage," Charles says. "I play tricks with her. Sometimes she'll lay her clothes out to dress and I might take part of them and hide them some place, where she can't find them. She's running around looking for them and I will swear I don't know where they were. Sometimes she doesn't know when I'm serious or not."

"I'd rather have her with me than anybody I know," Charles reflects. "That's the truth. I've told her that. I don't neglect her in public. I show her the same emotions in public that I do when we're at home."

"Feelings," Pauline muses. "I can appreciate all of that, because I do the same for him."

"I have to ask her sometimes, to remind me to do that," Charles adds, "but I try to do all those things."

"When my son came along I had more responsibility," Charles says. "I was a different person. My wife, as an adult, can take care of herself, but when you got a baby, you must feed it. The baby would suffer if I didn't take my responsibility seriously. This was a different life altogether."

"It didn't make a big change as far I was concerned," Pauline adds. "It was kind of a smooth transition. It really didn't change much because we shared the work. There was more joy and fun, you know, for the family. We didn't care for a lot of activities outside the house. By that I mean like going to clubs and a lot of dances and things like that. My personality was somewhat like his in that respect. We kind of liked being more reserved, yet enjoying each other. I'm sure that has been very important in our marriage—whether you enjoy each other, being with each other at all times. Oh, we have had some rough times, too. When I say rough, I don't mean fussing and leaving home. I'm just talking about disagreements between us. We agree to disagree."

"The biggest thing we argue about is what she said," Charles explains. "She'll say, 'I said this' and I'll say, 'Well, I didn't hear you say that, you didn't say that.' Then we argue about that. That's really all. I mean, that sounds unbelievable, but that's what it is. She'll just stop talking about it and I try to carry it on but I don't have anybody to carry it on with so I soon stop."

"It was fortunate that I would meet a person with a personality similar to mine," Pauline adds.

"I'll tell how she's different," Charles adds. "I'll try things. Even cooking for example. I do most of the cooking. She cooks very well, but she'll cook the same thing over and over and over. I like variety."

"Yeah, he likes a variety," Pauline chimes in. "He enjoys cooking because he loves eating. I've always said any man that can cook or help out, that's great. It doesn't have to be the woman's job."

"She's more apprehensive," Charles says. "She's reluctant to take chances and I'll take chances. Sometimes I have to kind of push her along or urge her along to do it. Grudgingly, she'll do it. She's a balancing force to my aggressiveness. She's a mellowing force to hold me back a little bit and I need that sometimes. If I didn't have this aggressiveness we would be in the Stone Age."

"I doubt that," Pauline answers. "We'll tease back and forth about who's the boss, but deep down there is not really a boss, yet I respect his aggressiveness.

"When you care about someone a lot, in love with someone as I am with Charles," Pauline continues, "you have a certain amount of jealousy. I've been able to control it, and he has not given me any reason to feel otherwise. I've never felt that I needed to worry about that because I know how I am with myself when I'm away from him."

"I talk about her to almost all my friends," Charles says. "When they meet her for the first time they already know about her. I do that for one main reason, to deter them from getting ideas about what I may do. We'll have that little wall between us, because I've talked so much about her. They don't believe anything will come between us. I try to stay apart so that I won't get to that point where I lose control."

"The good part is, I'm glad somebody else sees him as a person that they would flirt with," Pauline explains. "It is up to him if he wants to carry it out. There have been times that some people would like or needed to flirt with him, but it has never been anything to worry about."

"I couldn't handle it if she had an affair, for this reason," Charles explains. "I put so much energy trying not to get involved in an affair. I've put so much energy into this marriage that I'd be disappointed if she did get involved. The main reason is because ladies generally get emotionally involved in affairs. They concentrate about it more, they think about it more, it's not a spur-of-the-moment thing like it is with a man. I'm not saying that she should forgive me if I have one, but a man can have an affair and he might not remember the woman's name the next day. A lady is more attached. It's an expression of love for ladies, generally. It would end my marriage.

"One of the greatest compliments that a person can give his mate," Charles continues, "is to say, 'You're my best friend.' So one day I told her that. Boy! She got mad. 'I'm not your best friend! I'm your wife.'"

"That's true," Pauline adds. "He was just saying it so casual like this is just my friend, and I felt like, I'm his wife!"

"She is really my friend," Charles continues. "A lot of times, I'll say this is my best friend, Pauline, and then I pause and say she's also my wife. One time while working at the post office I came home dirty. We had only been married about a couple of months. I was working at night. When I came home she was in the bed. I washed my hands and took my wedding band off and put it on the sink. I got in the bed. She said, 'Where is the ring? You didn't want somebody to know you were married!' So she shows some jealousy sometimes. I had to straighten her out.

"She is more sensitive than I am," Charles continues. "She was more sensitive early on than she is now. She probably understands me now. She's more comfortable being intimate than she used to be. Oh man, she used to dress in the closet."

"I still do," Pauline chimes in. "From the beginning, I'm shy and bashful when it comes to intimacy—especially bedroom intimacy. After you know the touchy spots with your husband, you learn through the years how to deal with them and try to get more relaxed. Through the years he's taught me a lot, so I feel very relaxed now.

"He is not too sensitive," Pauline continues, "but it's enough that I know when he is. Sometimes men are sensitive, but they want you to think that they're not. He doesn't want me to think he is, but I can tell. After forty years you can show a little sensitivity, but he's done well with it. Fortunately, both of us came from religious families and we were already kind of molded. We've always worshiped together, so that helped a lot. We're believers, but we also know that you can believe but you must also do, to get prayers answered."

"God doesn't do all the things that we want," Charles explains. "People try to write God's job description. If something good happens we say God did it. If something bad happens, we say the devil did it. God has given us the ability to answer our own prayers. For example, if I don't drink water, I can pray until I'm blue in the face, but I'll die. God's not going to give me water because I've been provided with the intellect to go out and get the water I need. I use this in all aspects of my life. If I'm looking for a job I must prepare myself for the job. It wouldn't be fair for God to give me a job, and I haven't done anything. I am always mindful of this. We've been praying to feed the hungry. The hungry haven't been fed. They're dying and we still pray. We have to do. God's given us the intellect, the ability to share what we have, and we don't. I thank God every day for giving me the ability to sustain myself."

"I just can't imagine what it would be like without religion or faith or having a Supreme Being to pray to," Pauline adds.

"Action takes action," Charles explains. "I can say I love you one hundred times—it may not mean anything. But your actions demonstrate whether you love somebody or not. Action takes commitment. I'll tell anybody who gets married that you got to work at making your marriage work. Work together and make it work. It's going to require a lot of work and it's not just going to happen. You must be interested in the other person's welfare just like you are in your own. You got to share responsibility. You must help cook, clean up, wash—whatever you must do. You must do all those things together."

"And you must not let your mind wonder about outside the marriage," Pauline adds, "or being intimate or whatever else could come between you. You got to know how to be strong and push those things out of your mind and out of your marriage. Because temptation is really great, and it can destroy the marriage."

13
THROUGH THICK AND THIN

MARY AND RUPERT FEREBEE

Married November 13, 1946 · Currituck, North Carolina

103

Daddy had a big farm, which he was giving up," Mary begins. "We were moving from Pasquontank to Currituck. I met the girl that moved out of the house we moved in. Through her I met Rupert's sister and then I met him. I was eighteen and he was nineteen or twenty. When I met him he was going with someone else. I'm not the type of girl to butt in on another person's man. I spoke to him and went on about my business, but he kept pursuing me."

"She seemed like a quiet girl," Rupert adds. "It seemed like I could make it with her, so I tried to grab her."

"I didn't know a thing about him," Mary says. " I met him through his sister. We'd chat, and he'd try to get me and my girlfriend to go with him and his friend. I said nothing doing, because to me they were strangers. Another time he saw me standing at the bus stop. He comes over and talks to me. The next couple of weeks he was gone. He told me he was going into the service. He asked me if I would marry while he was in the service and I told him no. I had no plans of marriage. He asked me would I think of waiting on him. I said, 'I'll think about it but I really don't know you yet.'"

"I was in the army eighteen months," Rupert chimes in. "We courted mostly through writing."

"Wait for him!" Mary exclaims. "I love you and I want you to be my wife and all this crap. I was writing him back, but he had girlfriends. I really wasn't interested. I just liked boys as friends, not as boyfriends."

"I didn't want nobody else but her," Rupert admits. "I didn't like the service too much. We would sit around there and sleep like you was in jail. I wrote her a letter every other day. When I got back, I went straight to her home. She didn't live no more than about two miles and a half from me."

"He knocked on the door, came in the house, and we sat down and talked," Mary recalls. "His writing sounded sort of good, but I'm from the old school and everything a person says is not always right. They write what they think you want to hear. We stayed in the house and talked and talked."

"I couldn't find a job around there," Rupert adds. "I decided to go to New York and ask her to come with me. I knew she was going to say no and she did. I said, 'I promise to marry you before I leave.' I tried to force her to go, but she didn't want to go."

"He was very demanding," Mary points out. "He wanted to marry me and I said, 'no.' He got hot! I said, 'I want to finish school.' I don't like for nobody to act like they own me. When they do that, they're pushing me away from them because nobody owns me, I own myself. One day on my way to school, he told me to get in the car and come to town with him. He said he would take me to school. I let him sweet talk me and he took me straight to the doctor's office to get the blood test. He said, 'We can get the blood test and then we can get married later.' He knew what he was doing. I was the stupid one. I didn't know that you had to get married within ten days of the blood test. Because he had been in the service he was a little smarter than I was when it came to worldly things. I said, 'Why is it that we have to take a test now? We're not getting married.' When the doctor came back, I said, 'How long does this test last?' He said, 'You have to be married within ten days.' I yelled, 'Ten days! I didn't tell you I would marry you in ten days!' He looked at me with that little funny smile. Sho' nuff, within the ten days, we got married. We got married on a Wednesday. At first, I didn't want to marry him, to be honest.

"My daddy told me, if I thought that I could make it with him, he didn't see nothing wrong with it," Mary continues. "But be sure because when you make your bed hard you got to lie in it. Rupert came to the house that Sunday, and I still hadn't gotten it together. He came back on Monday. I said, 'Well all right, I guess I will marry you.' I liked him a lot, but I don't think it had really gotten into love. We hadn't been together that long. You can like a person, but to really love them, you have to grow into that."

"I don't think I really loved her," Rupert says, "not like I do now."

"Infatuation," Mary cautions, "that's all it was, infatuation.

"I wanted to base my marriage on what I had seen from my parents," Mary continues. "I saw love and humbleness, caring, no arguments—just a happy life. My parents were very lovable, although my mother died when she was forty-eight and I was thirteen. They were very lovable and taught us children to love one another. We couldn't fight each other. I'd never seen my father raise his hand to my mother, nor my mother to him. They wouldn't even allow us to say 'devil' or 'liar.' We had to say 'bad man' or 'storyteller.' My father was a preacher's son, so that made him kind of different.

"The third night we were married, Rupert went out and got drunk! Got drunk as a fish. I wasn't with him, so when he knocked on the door, I wouldn't open it for him. My daddy got up and opened it. Rupert came to live with me because if it hadn't been that way I wouldn't have married him because Dad didn't have nobody to take care of him."

"I tried to be a nice husband," Rupert says, "I tried to be. I tried to treat my family nice. My Daddy, he didn't hardly stay home too much. He worked for the Welfare Assistance Program— it's something like welfare. They send you off, you work, you make money, and then you go somewhere else and work. That's the kind of job that Daddy had. It was no more than going around digging people's ditches, when they farm. That's all I ever knew Dad to do. Mama took care of us. But Mama had fourteen children. I was number two. Number one died before I was born."

"When he came into the house," Mary recalls, "I said, 'Oh Lord, what have I gotten myself into?' What did I get myself into, a hornet's nest. I never liked people that drank. I never went with nobody, as a boyfriend, that drank. I didn't know he drank until that night. I didn't know nothing about annulment. Divorce, I didn't want that. I've seen it where people get drunk and beat their wives and I didn't want that."

"I was messing around with some of my friends in Elizabeth City, that I'd not seen in a long time," says Rupert. "They said, 'Come on man, let's go to the movies.' I said, 'No man, I got to go home.' They said, 'Come on!' I went on to the movies and he had this little old pint bottle and we was nipping it in the movies. I didn't know what was going to happen that night because when she gets mad, she's mad."

"He was more afraid of my father than he was of me that night," offers Mary.

"He'd never seen me drunk," Rupert admits. "I felt really bad, facing him."

"I let him sleep it off," says Mary. "When my father opened the door, he crawled in there crying, he was sorry, and all this kind of carrying on. He couldn't talk to me that night because I didn't hear him. The next morning we talked, and I told him if he ever did that again, we're calling it quits, because I was finished. I did not want no husband to go out and get drunk. He said he wouldn't do it again and he didn't until our kids was born. When our kids was born he got wild, again.

"I was raised without a mother, just a father," Mary continues. "Family, they don't tell you nothing. They didn't talk to you. This is the type of environment that I came up in. You really wasn't outspoken enough to tell nobody or let them know really what was happening out there. Everything was hush-hush. My sister couldn't tell me nothing because I don't think she was ever told nothing. Parents back then didn't believe in talking. I used to hear my mother and father talk. They would say, so-and-so broke her leg, or they heard from London. I'm wondering what is all this about! Broke a leg means she's having a baby and heard from London means they heard that she was pregnant. They didn't tell us nothing."

"I met up with the wrong crowd," Rupert offers. "Met up with the wrong crowd that drank and did some dope. My friends were in Queens and it was a Saturday night. I said, 'We don't need to go to that place.' But we went in anyway. After a while this lady came out of a room and took a cigarette—I thought it was a cigarette—and lit it. I took a puff. That's not what it was! They kept on blowing that stuff and it felt like my head was turning! When they said a party, I didn't go any more."

"God loves truth," states Mary adamantly "and my husband didn't calm down to be himself until his latter forties. He started acting like a real husband. I mean going to work and coming home to family. But by this time I did love him. Love is like a child growing up. Love has to grow. It don't come overnight. I had grown to love him.

"I am a good wife to him. I love him, take care of him, and do whatever I have to do to make him happy. He doesn't have to be ashamed to bring someone in unexpected. We go places together. Oh, I've changed quite a bit. I have learned how to be patient, to accept life, and accept him as he is. After you get a certain age, you're not changing. Don't let nobody tell you different. Isn't no way in the world I would trade him for somebody else, even with all his faults.

"Rupert has Alzheimer's. A lot of times it aggravates me, but I'm learning how to handle it, to deal with it. I don't really think he knows what he's doing, what he's saying, or how he's acting.

Therefore, I have learned to be a better wife to him. I forgot about those days, the bad days. Daddy and I are mellow. He has mellowed, and we are having a good life. I'd much rather have the rough life when I was young than to have it now."

"I've changed," Rupert admits. "I'm older and I'm not as strong as I used to be. Some mornings I get up and I feel weaker and then sometimes I feel stronger. In my young days, I'd say when I was around about 65, I would feel a lot spryer than I do now. I can't think as good. I can't stand too much noise, like lots of children."

"He hasn't changed that much," Mary says. "Rupert is still hot-tempered. He gets angry very quick."

"And if she says something that makes me angry," Rupert adds, "I'd just walk on out of the house. I'll see you later. Walk right on out."

"Then we'd come back and talk about it afterwards," Mary says.

"Yeah," he says.

"Because you can't hear each other when you're both angry," Mary continues. "I believe in God, and any problems that we have we take it to God and pray over it. He'll straighten it out, regardless of what it is. We had to go to church. It was instilled in me that we must go to church. I've always been in church singing in the choirs. Believe it or not, I thought I got him out of the church."

"Before we got married, he'd go to church. Because sometimes he used to come and take me to church. I don't bother him too much. Every once in a while I'd say, come on and go to church. He says, 'No, I don't want to go.' Seeing couples come in the church together started me to thinking, why is it that my husband can't come to church? He can go play bingo, but he don't want to go to church."

"If I'm going to go to church on Sunday," Rupert offers, "and then go that following week and go to a poker game, play cards or bingo or go to a casino or something, it's no need of me playing with God like that. That's the way I felt and that's how come I didn't join. Lots of times she tells me, she says, 'Why don't you come on and go to church?' I say I'm going to bingo this week so why should I go to church? I didn't want to be a hypocrite."

"I don't bug him," Mary admits. "I don't say a word to him. The only thing I say to him is don't ask me to go. If he wants to go and that's what he enjoys, fine. I enjoy church, he enjoys bingo. I believe that something is happening, whether he's praying or what, something is happening, because the man used to go to bingo just about every night."

"Hard luck," Rupert laughs. "I'm going to tell you the truth, it's hard luck."

"You should be ashamed of yourself," Mary insists. "What he means by hard luck is that he hasn't been winning.

"Lord's talking to you," Mary continues. "He's trying to tell you something. You won't listen."

"I agree with you there," he says.

"I didn't know you looked at it that way," Mary answers.

"It's something I'm not doing right," Rupert continues.

"Playing bingo! Because that's part of the devil's work, that's why you don't win," Mary points out.

"I pray, Lord, take it from me," Rupert admits. "Take the bingo from me, that and the smoking."

"There is a change that came about in there somewhere," Mary smiles. "That man used to go to bingo every night."

14
GIVE AND TAKE

BERNESE AND ARCHIE MEYER

Married September 4, 1958 · North Augusta, South Carolina

O n this page of pink I leave this spot of ink, Romeo.' He wrote that in my autograph book. I was in elementary school and he was a big time senior. We would visit the high school and the seniors rarely paid any attention to the little prefreshman," Bernese says. "What he wrote intrigued me."

"I wrote what I considered to be a normal sort of thing you put in an autograph book for a prefreshman. She was cute, but she was a little young for me," says Archie.

"He was off to college and we didn't see each other for a while," says Bernese. "He went to Morehouse College and I went to Morris Brown—that's where we rekindled our friendship. One day he came on campus to give a friend of mine a ride home to North Augusta, South Carolina. She was not on the honor roll that semester, so she couldn't go, but lucky for me, I was an honor student and got to ride to South Carolina with him. That's how it all started.

"Every thing was predestined for us," Bernese continues. "I was supposed to be an early admission student at Bennett College in Greensboro, North Carolina, but I didn't want to miss my senior year, so I opted not to go. I chose to complete my senior year and go to college the next year. I had seen Archie a couple of times here and there, being from the same general area, but nothing clicked. I even introduced him to my roommate because I knew he would be safe with her. She was safely in love with her high school boyfriend, who was in the service.

"I was dating the cocaptain of the football team and that was big time for a little country girl. I was playing it from both angles. One time I was sitting in the front seat with one of Archie's friends and he was in the back seat with my roommate. Looking through the mirror at them, it dawned on me that that I may not want this to continue," Bernese admits. "This went on my entire freshman year and then at the beginning of my sophomore year things started happening. We started dating; it was like a whirlwind. Everything seemed to have fallen in place. There was no more roommate for him and no more cocaptain of the football team for me. We were a twosome from that point on, as if nothing else had ever happened in the past.

BERNESE AND ARCHIE MEYER
IN 1966, AFTER TWELVE YEARS
OF MARRIED LIFE.

"We got engaged my sophomore year and he asked me to marry him."

"There were a few intervening things that happened. I had already graduated, was working, and from time to time returned to Atlanta to stay with my cousin," says Archie. "I told my cousin, I'm going to see if this country girl can cook. So I brought her over to my cousin's house, who was rooming in a house with one of the professors that was on sabbatical. I guess I enjoyed her cooking, because it wasn't too long after that that I asked her to marry me. Bernese was a homegirl. She was raised like my mother was raised, to take care of their families. I like to eat at home, so her being a good cook was one of the major factors in my decision."

"I left school, got married, and went with Archie."

"If you were a black male you either preached, taught school, worked for the government, or sold insurance. I sold insurance," Archie offers. "If you were lucky you would get a job with a future. Eventually, I went to Washington and worked with the Home Finance Agency that later became Housing & Urban Development. I was reassigned to Fort Worth, Texas, and that is where we started raising a family."

"I was giddy and in love," Bernese beams. "I had a cousin who would say, 'If you just marry the man, if you're lucky enough to be in love with him that's fine, but if you're not, it doesn't make any difference.' I wanted somebody responsible and God-fearing, but I also want to be in love. I was lucky, I got the brass ring. When we got married, we vowed that if we had a problem with the other, we would talk about it and resolve it before going to bed. It is the one thing that has sustained our marriage. I'm more in love with my husband now than I was when we married. We have stayed up late at night to talk about things."

"We came through during a period when you went to school, got a job, and then married," Archie explains. "There were high moral standards and expectations that you would get married by a certain age come hell or high water. Then you'd stay together. Divorces were taboo."

"If you were lucky enough to be with someone that you were really fond of, that helped. I was in love and so happy," says Bernese. "We were from the same background. You found someone, then dated, and, if you saw that you were going to have a future together, you'd get married. If you didn't you'd move on. It's a different story now. People can date seven or eight years. When that happens it becomes too much of a way of life. I'm glad I came along when I did."

"My cousin loved Bernese from the first time she met her. That was a big plus because anything that my cousin said to my mother about Bernese was absolutely good. When my mother met her, she fell in love with her. They had a special relationship. My parents seldom had serious disagreements about things. They worked to keep their marriage together and to raise their nine children. That's how it lasted."

"My parents were divorced, but Archie promised my family that I would finish school and they believed him. We always knew that I would finish and we worked towards that. At first we traveled, and when we got to a stationary point I finished school. In our day, certain things were expected of you. You got married and had children. To raise them in a loving environment, where the children are shown that the parents love each other, is one of the best things you can do for your children. Each child brings its own uniqueness to a situation. Having children enhanced our

THE MEYERS POSE FOR A FAMILY PHOTO DURING THE WEDDING OF THEIR ELDEST SON, ARCHIE JR., IN 1994. FROM LEFT: RHAYCHELLE, ARRICK, ARCHIE SR., ARCHIE JR., BERNESE, TONYA, AND ERICA.

relationship because we shared the responsibility. He worked and I raised the children with his help, and his help was tremendous.

"When I went back to school I had his assistance and luckily my mother was at a point in her career that she could help," says Bernese. "Even after my mother returned home I would be able to go places, to conventions, and Archie would take care of the kids. My friends would remark, 'Oh my goodness, your husband is going to stay at home?' He's always made me feel as if the care of our children was his responsibility too. There was never a time when I couldn't go someplace that I really wanted to that he wouldn't look after the children while I was away. That had been a real plus. However, I elected to give up my job so I could take care of other things so he would be free to do what he needed. When I did work outside of the home it would be at a point where we had help with the children and the house. I've only worked a total of eight years during the time we've been married. Our marriage was more traditional, where the wife did certain things and had particular responsibilities.

"I don't care how good something is, there's always conflict; therefore, compromise is necessary. However, when you have that underlying commitment and respect, it's easier to do," admits Bernese. "If I didn't have some of the things that really make me glow when I think of Archie, it would be more difficult. It's not magic."

"For a marriage to be successful there has to be some give and take. She knows when to take and I know when to give and when I take she gives."

"It may sound like magic, but it's really not. We have been willing to be what the other expects. The willingness to see from the other's perspective without being angry or hostile about it. We do it because there's something greater than either of us, there's a 'we.' We even still show affection," Bernese offers.

"Cuddle," Archie smiles.

"We still do that and I enjoy it. We try to find a little time that we can spend to ourselves. It doesn't always have to be a sexual thing. It can just be being close to each other. Sometimes we'll sit for thirty minutes, an hour, and don't talk . . . just be together," Bernese smiles affectionately.

15
WEATHERING THE STORMS

J E R I   A N D   A D E L L   M I L L S

Married December 10, 1961 · Los Angeles, California

My dad didn't want me to go to an all-night movie, so the only way I was going to get to go was to find my brother who was on the inside. I said, 'Daddy if I can get in and find Horace, can I go?' He didn't think that was going to happen. With a little box-shaped plastic purse in my hand I walked up to the window. At first I thought it was a white guy until I got closer. Gee, he's black, I got it made. I threw my hair, explained the circumstances, and offered to leave my purse," says Jeri.

"It was the Starlight Drive-In and I was the person that sells tickets. She came in and I couldn't believe my eyes, she was looking so pretty. I was excited," Adell admits. "When she told me that she would leave her purse, I said 'Uh-uh, you don't have to leave nothing and you can have this whole damn movie!' That was it for me."

"There was no first-time attraction for me. It was senior night and I was already excited in terms of being with my friends at the movies and graduating," says Jeri.

"They came back that same night and I let them in the movie. I didn't get her phone number until two weeks later. Then we began to talk," Adell says. "It was about three weeks before I asked her out on a date. On our first date I must have had her entire family with us. We went to Tyler State Park, and at that particular time it wasn't integrated, so the white policeman ran us off the grounds. We were in the wrong section, so we left and went to the colored section. Her family was escorting her. She had her brother, her sister, and her two cousins. I was enjoying myself because I was enjoying her. She was supposed to be babysitting."

"That was the only way I could go that day," Jeri chimes in.

"I just took the entire gang, because that was the only way she was going to get to go," Adell continues.

"The relationship began to get stronger and stronger and it just kept getting better," Adell recalls.

"We talked a lot on the phone. In those days guys that lived in the dormitory would have twenty minutes on the phone and then had to give it up to somebody else. Through our conversations I knew he was a football player, a starter, and played tight end. I begin thinking, here I am going to be a little freshman and I have a junior football player interested in me! Boy! It really was a big deal! Over the summer before I went to school we became an item.

"He was not like other guys. I'll never forget this," Jeri muses. "During our first kiss, he was rubbing me on my arms and told me I was soft like a rabbit—that was sincere and honest. Another thing, one night we were outside in the front yard, and I told him I was real cold. That was my coy way of wanting him to put his arms around me. Instead of him picking up on that clue, he said, 'Well okay, let me get you in the house.'

"I honestly have to say he more or less grew on me," Jeri admits. "At the beginning I had no real feelings one way or the other. I just liked the way he treated me. He treated me like a lady. He was very sincere and gentle."

"Jeri stood apart from other ladies. There wasn't any phoniness; it was all 'real.' That's what caught my attention. By being a farm boy, a country boy, I always looked at those things, being natural. Then her smile—she had a glow and you would have to go a long way to find a sincere smile like that."

"After being together for three years there was a rocky period," Jeri says. "My mama told me, frankly, that she thought I was getting too serious about him. We were seeing too much of each other, and she wanted me to finish school. In those days she thought I would get pregnant, and Lord knows I wasn't even intimate, but I knew it was coming. I went to him and told him that we needed a little space. He was hurt, but I didn't tell him that my mom had suggested it."

"I kind of felt like she let me down, sort of turned her back on me," Adell says. "She knew how a man would feel, going with a lady for four or five years and hadn't been intimate with her. At that particular time, young men of my status were sexually active. I refused to be sexually active with her, because she was going to to be my wife."

"I was giving him the freedom to be active, to be intimate with somebody else. One day I went to my aunt's house, whose friend lived next door to the woman Adell was dating. While visiting her one night, I saw Adell's car at the neighbor's house. The lights were on in the duplex.

The windows were down even though it was summer! "I thought I smelled fried chicken or something. We knocked on this woman's door, planning to leave flowers for the woman next door. They wouldn't come to the door!"

"I wasn't there," Adell exclaims. "I keep telling her, these thirty years, I wasn't there, I wasn't there! I was over at another lady's house. I just left my car there."

"He'd never leave his car. I think that relationship was the result of hurt feelings. At the same time I was hurt because Adell was with someone else. A little bit later on he called me and told me he had decided to move to California. He said, 'My brother is out there and I need to get away. I'd really like to see you before I go.' Though we weren't together the love never stopped. I was really trying to do what my mom was saying," Jeri explains. "The next step was going to be intimacy and I couldn't handle that without being married. My mom told me things like, 'If you have a baby, you'll be put in a ditch.' And I could envision myself in a ditch alone, with a child.

"He never really proposed. It was always assumed from our discussions that we would get married. We talked and planned our life. We planned a boy and a girl. I would stay home with the children while he worked. We wanted our children to be two or three

JERI AND ADELL ON A
DATE WHILE ATTENDING
TEXAS COLLEGE IN TYLER, TEXAS.

years apart. When he told me he was going to California and that he wanted me to come with him, it was May. That September I didn't go back to school, I went to California."

"It was a justice of the peace wedding," says Adell.

"My parents at the time couldn't have afforded a big wedding, so we decided that we would simplify things," Jeri says. "My aunt gave us a reception in California. My mother and father were disappointed, because at that time they couldn't afford the air fare."

"Our life was like a storybook," Jeri says. "I stayed at home and took care of the kids and Adell worked at the University of California. He had a good position there. I had the kids right away; three children were born within four years. There was an adjustment period for sure. Our life started to change when I was pregnant with the third child, which was totally unexpected. We had already had our boy and girl and then another daughter comes along. My daughter refers to herself as 'Mom and Dad's mistake.' I was five months pregnant before I realized it. The unexpected pregnancy caused me to act sort of funny. He would go bowling with his friends and I didn't want him to go. It escalated to the point that I took the two children and packed them in the car and ran away.

"I went where I thought he would never find me," Jeri continues. "The first place he would look would be at my two aunts' and then at my godmother's house. I had been planning this and I didn't tell either one of the three where I was going. I ended up at his sister's house and she promised not to tell Adell and she didn't—sort of. At three o'clock in the morning, the phone rang. I'd gotten the kids bathed and settled down. I was sleeping on the sofa and could hear my sister-in-law's conversation. She said, 'Wherever Jeri and those kids are, they are all right.' Adell knew right away where I was and by sunrise he was there."

"She's blood," exclaims Adell. "Blood will always let you know. I called all of her relatives and friends and they hadn't seen or heard from her. I was worried because she was pregnant and had the other two kids. After I called everyone else, I called my sister, because if she had not seen her, she would help me find Jeri."

"I had to get accustomed to him. We both have strong personalities, but when it really gets down to it, he's more dominant. I would like to think of myself as being dominant, but over the years

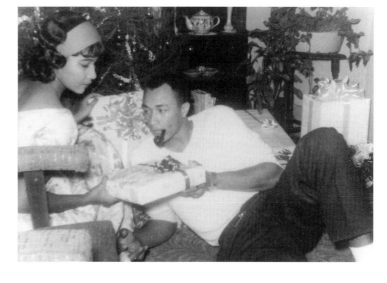

JERI AND ADELL SHARE GIFTS ON ONE OF THEIR FIRST CHRISTMASES AS A MARRIED COUPLE IN THE EARLY 1960S.

it's too much of a challenge to overpower him. I found that out early. There are times that I'm assertive, but it would take too much out of him to not be in control. I use my leadership skills in other roles, like on my job, and I've been a leader everywhere else but here," she laughs.

"It's just certain things she expects of me," Adell explains. "I bring home the paycheck and she expects that to happen. She expects me to take care of other things, like making sure gas is in her car. By saying that I am in control means that both of us come to an understanding. She has her own ideas and I always seek her input. It doesn't mean that I'm just going to sit and tell her what to do.

"It's one thing that makes us stay together more than anything," says Adell. "Anytime you get upset or mad, go away. But before you go to bed that night, resolve all conflict, because you don't know if you are going to wake up the next morning."

"I've ignored that rule," Jeri responds. "He's never ignored it. I've ignored it, particularly in the last five years when hormonal changes started."

"We made that pledge, maybe ten or fifteen years ago," Adell explains. "Probably church is the area we have the most disagreement."

"We're different religions," Jeri says. "I'm Presbyterian, he's Baptist. My mom was Baptist, my dad was Church of the Living God. I can recall times when my dad questioned my mom about Baptist things and she questioned him about his church. Later she went to his church, like I went to Adell's church for awhile. I wouldn't call it disagreements, but we have philosophical differences. Baptist folks meet so much, three or four nights a week. I question him about the necessity of that."

"I mess with them Presbyterians, all the time, even my boss. My boss and Jeri go to the same church. I tell him he needs to come to the Baptist church to get some religion," Adell laughs. "When I go to Jeri's church, the service starts at eleven o'clock and we're out by twelve o'clock. It doesn't seem like we had any service. It's interesting, it's real interesting. It's interesting the type of service they have. Sometimes the preacher gets into it and you want to say 'Amen,' but you can't."

"That's been our biggest difference; however, we support each other," Jeri says.

"I tease her, but I go to her church too."

"It's our desire to want to be together in spite of the difficulties. You've got to want to," says Jeri. "If we were looking for an excuse we could have found one with three children at Hampton University at the same time. That would have financially broken us apart because we were in a financial bind for several years, trying to keep them in school. But instead of letting that pull us apart, which it could have easily done, we committed ourselves to seeing this thing through.

"When domestic problems occur, your mate is a reminder of those problems," Jeri continues. "You think, 'I can do better by myself,' that kind of attitude. If the mate is not around, then you are not reminded about the problems. If you're looking for a reason, finances can do it. If anything, maybe it pulled us closer."

"And one of the main things that you have to do is, I know you need a lot of prayer, but you sho'nuff have to laugh," Adell says.

"We have never had a marriage that crowded each other," Jeri says. "We've given each other space. Since we've been married we have spent time away from each other. I need to miss him being here, miss him taking out the trash or having to put gas in my car. I need to miss that and then I can appreciate it better. I think I could handle a one-night stand," Jeri says with hesitation. "If it's just somebody he happened to see out there and had too much to drink or it was a big storm and they just happened to be there and it happened, that's one thing. But two or three years with the same old person, I'm not sure I could handle that, because that's treading into my territory."

"Some things are not necessary to tell, because it's going to come out sooner or later," Adell explains.

"I would tell everything, because that's part of my nature," Jeri says.

"I think that's another part of our relationship that has weathered the storm," Adell admits. "We have been truthful to each other. When you start hiding things, I think that is when the truth explodes in your face. If you are involved in a long-term relationship outside of the marriage, that means you're not satisfied with your mate. If you are taking care of her needs, emotionally and physically, and she is taking care of yours, you don't have time to go no place."

"One time, I was listening to a friend. She tells me, 'You see these numbers around here, honey, they're calling them.' She was putting all kinds of things in my mind. And sure enough, I was washing clothes and this number falls out of Adell's shirt pocket. There was no name or anything. Oh, I debated about calling that number for at least three hours. It finally got the best of me, and I dialed it. It was Purina Dog Chow. I thought this must be a mistake, and I dialed the number the second time—same thing. He was working as an animal technician at the University of California in Berkeley, so that explained it. I learned my lesson. During the last five years I had one hormonal question of jealousy and we talked about it and his response satisfied me.

"It's better to love someone than to be in love," Jeri explains. "I know I'm bigger now and I've gained more weight, my hair is getting gray and I have a double chin. He's lost his hair and the lines are coming in. We continue to be attracted to each other but it's not the same as sexual attraction. That part is not there anymore, so you must substitute that for something more real, because basically that same person is there."

"She put on a little weight, but I look at the overall picture. I love that smile she has—it carries me a long way. She has put on a little weight, but I don't have a problem with it. If anybody else has a problem with it, that's just tough luck."

"Our attitudes have changed too," Jeri admits. "Once my children finished school and college, I moved into more demanding jobs in my career. When I came home, I was mentally exhausted and Adell was too. He would go to the den, take a seat, and put on the TV. I'm upstairs doing the laundry, the cooking, and the whole bit. We had a little rocky time there for a while. I told him, 'It won't hurt you to fold these clothes.' I would put them in front of him and he'd just keep letting them sit there. And I'd just keep putting them in front of him. Sometimes the clothes would stay in the basket for seven or eight days. And then he'd start asking, 'Where's my stuff?' I would reply, 'In the basket to be folded.' Finally, he started folding clothes. This tug-of-war about helping in the house went on for about seven years. But now he'll pick up, vacuum, fold the clothes, or do whatever he can to help. I practiced the Gandhi treatment on him, passive resistance."

"I was cooling out. Given her responsibilities outside of the home and the times she worked beyond five o'clock, I thought I should pitch in and start working with her. I still don't do as much as I could. Sometimes I think that men don't pay attention to the sensitivities of women like they should, as is evident in this particular situation," Adell admits. "I think that's been one of my weak points."

"I'm satisfied with the level of his participation," Jeri says.

"I really think our obstacles have strengthened us," Jeri adds. "They could have destroyed us, but we just had the desire that we wouldn't let it."

"I think if I had it to do all over again I wouldn't change a thing," Adell concludes.

16
Ready for Commitment

LOUISE MCKOY AND GEORGE SHIPMAN

Married December 22, 1948 · Clarkton, North Carolina

How would I tell my mother what I had to say?" George asks. "After dinner, I kept looking at the new baby girl, who was one year old. I was four years old. I looked at the baby in the crib and told my mama that this is the girl for me. My mother and Louise's mother were good friends," George recalls. "One Sunday afternoon, my mother and I went to visit her mother."

"He didn't know I was going to be his wife," Louise smiles. "He tells that story all the time. We're from the same city or shall I say small town. I knew him from Sunday school, but I didn't know him that well. I really didn't get to know him until he finished high school. I met him when he came by the house and for some reason he left something. I don't know whether that was deliberate or not. It gave him an opportunity to get back by the house. From that point, a relationship developed."

"I was testing an old theory that I created at four years old, to see if it would come true," George says. "When I looked at Louise, she looked like she wanted to go to college, so I said, 'Let me stick close and see what happens.' I was just testing it out to see if we could develop a relationship that would lead to something interesting. She was an attractive young lady and she had an outgoing personality. Those were the qualities I saw in her early in the relationship."

"George was a smart guy, tall and very thin. I was sort of tall, and I never wanted a fellow I could look down on, physically. My daddy was the superintendent of the Sunday school for many years. George used to work closely with my father for many years and I thought that anybody who went to church regularly was someone you could depend on and probably had some integrity. My parents got along rather well. I can't ever recall seeing or hearing them fussing; if so, they did it privately. My mother was a talkative person. She was stricter than my daddy. I got as much discipline from daddy as I did my mother. Daddy was a churchgoer and had Christian values. If he saw us doing something he thought we shouldn't, he would let us know."

"My parents went up to the sixth or seventh grade," says George. "They were very interested in their children getting more education than that. I think that was one of the things, especially, my

THE SHIPMANS IN
THE 1950S, DURING
THE EARLY YEARS OF
THEIR MARRIAGE.

mother impressed on me. That was one of the values passed on to me by the family. And if I'm going to get a college education, I certainly would like for my wife to have a college degree, too.

"We dated for seven, eight, or nine years," George explains. "I was a junior in college when she entered college. I kept a pretty good check on her by visiting her. She went to North Carolina Central University in Durham and I went to Livingstone College in Salisbury, North Carolina. In addition to her academics, she played basketball. She did so well that she was inducted into the North Carolina Central University Athletic Hall of Fame. I figured that I had made a pretty good choice."

"We dated for years," Louise agrees. "We dated before he went to the navy. I considered him 'just' a friend because he had other girlfriends too. I think because he was going to the navy he wanted to have someone special. For some reason I wasn't ready to settle down right then. I told him, 'When I do marry, I want to be a true, faithful wife.' I wasn't quite ready for that commitment."

"I was patient," says George. "I waited a couple of years. I was waiting for time to bring it into fruition," says George.

"It didn't come to fruition until we were working together at Booker T. Washington High School in Clarkton, North Carolina," Louise answers. "We got to know each other while we were teaching school. One day during the Christmas break, we drove down to Wilmington, North Carolina, to the home of a Methodist minister whom George knew. We couldn't find this minister anywhere, so we headed back home. While driving back, George said, 'I came down here to get married and I'm going to get married,' so he turned around and found a Baptist minister to whom he had sold insurance. The ceremony was held in his living room, the wife played the organ, and she and the daughter were our witnesses. That was our wedding.

"The first year we stayed with my parents, then the next year we moved out on our own," Louise continues. "That was the first time we had a home, furniture, and all of that. Where we lived, just a road or street divided us from the school. It was just a matter of walking across the road. Sometimes I would cook and sometimes mama would cook. The next year someone came in to give us a hand with cooking and the laundry because both of us were working. We worked there for several years, then he became a principal. Then we kept moving, moving, moving because he kept going from one principal position to another. When he moved to the first principal position they had to hire three persons to replace him."

"Eventually, I went to graduate school," George says. "I wanted to get a master's degree in North Carolina, but they weren't permitting blacks into the University of North Carolina, so I went to Boston University. Not all the institutions were open for blacks to get a doctoral degree, either. I was fortunate to have an opportunity to have helped desegregate George Peabody College in Nashville, Tennessee. It was an experiment to see if blacks could handle the doctoral work, and I successfully completed the program. We were guinea pigs."

"Six years into the marriage, we had a child," says George proudly. "It was a healthy experience having to focus on the child. Sometimes when there is no child, the husband and wife are too focused on themselves. When a child arrives, you must give up a little bit of that ego and focus on taking care of the child. That was a healthy experience.

"We tried to instill in him some of the values that we learned from our parents," George explains.

"I don't know that we planned it that way," Louise admits. "We knew he needed to go to church. We knew he had to go to school and we knew he needed to learn how to work."

"Then you look at the environment that he is in, which may be different from the environment in which you grew up," George continues.

"When we would see him doing something wrong," Louise points out, "we always said, 'We got to have a conference, we got to talk about this.' We always tried to instill in him to make wise decisions, because you'll have to suffer the consequences of your decisions. He heard this throughout his life."

"Our son, the Reverend Sheldon R. Shipman, is now the pastor of Wall Memorial A.M.E. Zion Church in Charlotte, North Carolina," Louise states proudly.

"He has been a minister for twenty years and is currently pursuing a doctor of ministry degree. He is married to Teresa McNair Shipman, an administrator for Mecklenburg Schools in Charlotte, North Carolina. They are the proud parents of twins, Joshua and Jamiel Shipman, and, of course, that makes us very happy and extremely proud grandparents.

"I'm a family person," Louise admits, "very outgoing and interested in people, always tending to others peoples' affairs and needs."

"That's for sure!" George chimes in. "My personality is a little different from hers. I'm not quite as effervescent as she is. I'm more reserved. I am more cautious. I ask a lot of questions. That may come from my training as an educator, that you don't take things for face value. You dig into them and find out about them before you make a commitment to them. I'm normally friendly and have the spirit of helping people.

"I think I have shown a great deal of respect for my wife," George says. "I've been a loving husband. Nothing is more important than being truthful. You can think you can get away with it by misrepresenting the truth, but that makes it very uncomfortable for you over time because you've got to remember the stories you told her, if it isn't the truth. If it's the truth, it comes back to you immediately. I believe in behaving in such a way the makes my mate feel like she is somebody special. If ever I get to the point where I don't make her feel she's special, the relationship is in trouble."

"I feel loved," Louise smiles, "because George still gives me roses, red roses. He is very considerate and thoughtful. I guess, maybe, he kind of lets me have my way about things. He knows that I like to buy a lot of things, and to keep me from buying a lot, sometimes, when I put on something I've had before, he'll say 'Honey, when did you get that new dress? I haven't seen that before!' You know, try to flatter me."

"My wife is a spendthrift," George adds. "If I want her to spend less on clothes then I try to motivate her by bragging on some of those clothes that are in the closet that she hasn't worn for three years. I say, 'I haven't seen you in that dress in ages, Sugar, why don't you wear that sometimes?'"

"I'll tell you one thing about George," says Louise. "He does not bother me that much. I can't remember him saying, 'Louise I don't think you need that.' He trusts me, so I love him for that, although I may need a plaque for staying with him for forty-eight years! We celebrate every anniversary."

"Some years ago, she bought a mattress for the bed," George says, "and the mattress we had was perfect!"

"And he's enjoying the mattress," Louise chimes in. "I still have common sense. I know when and when not to buy. There has been a turning point in our relationship since we have retired. Whereas George will get in the kitchen now, and suggest how something needs to be done. I don't think I need the suggestion after all these years, and I let him know that. But I let him know it in a nice way. I'll say, 'You have two hands!' and let him know that he could do it, if he likes to have it done another way."

"I just make suggestions sometimes," says George. "Our retirement was a turning point, because it put me in a relationship with my wife where I am home all the time, and that had not been the case before."

"Like cornbread," laughs Louise. "I try to make cornbread, and I hit and miss. I don't cook much; I'm not that kind of a "good" cook. He likes to suggest how something needs to be cooked, especially cornbread."

"Maybe I meddle a little more than I should at home, just because I'm here," George admits. "If I had been working like I've been doing most of my life, I wouldn't have time to do that. I guess I do make more suggestions now about things that are done, than I did before."

"I'm going to show him the meal, the flour, the eggs, the oil," Louise laughs. "I'm going to show him all the ingredients and let him try his hand. Sharing is important. I don't think that all the housework is just for the lady.

"While he was working, he didn't have time to deal with house things," Louise explains. "If he gets too involved, I'll say, 'I've been with you for over forty-some years, so don't begin trying, after more than forty years, to get that involved.'"

"I think I made a good adjustment," admits George. "I let her know what gets on my nerves, because if I don't let her know how it gets on my nerves then she won't know what she's doing that I don't like. I try to make her aware of it and do it in such a way that I'm not fussing but sharing the information. I would call that communication. If I don't communicate with her, she won't know. I try to understand why she behaves that way and be patient."

"Being around home and retired sometimes he may want to disagree about something, really disagree, but not be disagreeable," says Louise. "If it doesn't mean that much to me, I compromise. Compromise has a lot to do with giving and taking. You don't have to take all the time, but then you don't have to give all the time either. That's compromising. If you communicate, you may not have to do so much compromising because you have some kind of a mutual understanding."

"I have shown a great deal of respect for my wife," George points out. "I've been a loving husband. I have loved her for all these years. If there is something to be criticized—criticize in such a way that you're not belittling. She gives me consideration in so many instances. She cooks my meals, that's a consideration. Remembering my birthday, Father's Day, and other holidays—not just holidays, but any day. Saying things that motivate me. These are expressions of love. We have been in this relationship for almost fifty years and when we make it, I'll ask the Heavenly Father to give us fifty more years."

17
SUNSHINE AND SHADOWS

E. VIVIAN AND LOUIS WILLIAMS

Married June 14, 1943 · Atlanta, Georgia

I walked into class with my hair in braids and Lou was teaching Afro-American history in the absence of his professor," Vivian begins. "I didn't know one thing about Afro-American history. He asked me a question and I turned around and said I don't know what you're talking about. I don't know one thing about Afro-American history. After the shock of him calling on me, I sat down and started listening. I was very, very impressed with what he was telling the students and thought I had better listen."

"I was taken by her appearance and the friskiness she displayed," Lou admits. She was a frisky little something. Consciously or unconsciously, I think I was looking for a girlfriend. Given the way she carried herself—her ways and actions—I probably took some liking to her. At the time, I said something to get her attention and we struck up a friendship. I'd walk her home from school; that's how the relationship started."

"He would walk me home because he lived on campus and I didn't. My brothers used to pick me up but I didn't want them to pick me up all the time. I had five brothers and my oldest brother wouldn't let a boy come near me. They wanted to pick who would come home to visit me. I was more or less a little old tomboy."

"She was sheltered," Lou says.

"I was very much sheltered," Vivian admits. "My parents trusted Lou and my brothers were very impressed with him. He was the type of person they wanted me to meet. I had lots of male acquaintances," says Vivian. "Although I would flirt, there was peer pressure from girls. They would have thought I was a . . .

"I wasn't thinking about girlfriend or boyfriend for the first two years," Vivian recalls. "Lou was a friend. We talked about our families and would go to school activities. He was interesting. He had so much to talk about. He was very smooth, intelligent, a smooth talker."

"I should have been a lawyer," Lou smiles.

"At first the relationship was platonic," continues Lou. "We'd just chit-chat and carry on small conversation. While visiting her and walking her home, it eventually blossomed into a so-called romance. Then we would see each other regularly.

"In '41 my father passed," Lou says. "When I went home, I didn't go back to school that year. I stayed out and worked. Then in '42 I was drafted and went into the military. While in the army, I wrote her a letter, which was the beginning of this all. We resumed our contact. I asked about our relationship and seeing her again. I would get three-day passes and a furlough and go to Atlanta. Our relationship became more intense, but I don't remember her writing me back. I made numerous trips to Atlanta and would take the bus or train. After my first trip to Atlanta, I made up my mind to marry her."

"I was in love," Vivian says. "I wanted to see Lou, so my mother let me go visit him in Columbus. At that particular time, I was a majorette and we traveled to different cities with our school team. I was chaperoned very closely, but they knew about my boyfriend. They let me see Lou for a short time. I don't know whether Lou remembered this—he said, 'I'm going to marry you' and I said, 'You are? We'll see.' I kissed him; our first kiss was in Columbus, Georgia. Oh wow! He wrote wonderful love letters expressing how he loved me. We were real honest with one another."

"On one of my trips, maybe the last time, I went to visit her parents and asked for her hand in marriage," says Lou. "That was in the fall of '42. Then our wedding was set for June of '43. She didn't meet my family until after we got married. When I was in the army, I wasn't free to go as much as I wanted. Her folks, being as protective as they were, wouldn't allow her to go."

"We had wedding invitations and everything," Lou explains. "Then I got orders to report to the army special training course in Greensboro, North Carolina. It was the height of World War II and things were heating up. I called Vivian and she got busy. She called the Red Cross and they got active. I was summoned to the office by my commanding officer. The commanding officer said, 'Soldier, why didn't you tell anyone you were supposed to get married?' I said, 'I don't know sir.' He said, 'You go get yourself ready and we're going to put you on that train tonight.' That was on a Friday and the wedding was on that Saturday."

"The church was packed. It was the most beautiful wedding," Vivian muses. "Lou arrived on Saturday morning. The courthouse was closed, therefore we couldn't get our license. We weren't married legally. Very few knew that we weren't 'really' married, that was the beautiful part. Of course there were a lot of tears, we were young and didn't know if it would work out. We couldn't make love at all because he had to go back to training. We spent a few moments together, we kissed and embraced."

"They gave me a two-week pass after we married and that was the first time we made love," Lou chimes in.

"He gave me love, taught me love," Vivian smiles shyly. "I will never forget his tenderness. I was frightened, but it was tender. He had to be tender to keep the pain away. With his love and embraces it was one of the most beautiful experiences. The next time I was eager. To look at me, I was frisky and fast, but I had never been with a boy or man. Lou was my first. And then being old-fashioned, I never refused sex to Lou in anger. He was my husband. I was always ready for him. He always smelled good and he always talked sweet. I really fell in love with my husband."

"I held her spellbound," Lou smiles.

"My parents were very much in love," Vivian remembers. "They met as students at Tuskegee. My father had a very large family, thirteen. When his mother passed, his father married a cousin and they had thirteen

E. VIVIAN AT EIGHTEEN,

BEFORE SHE MARRIED.

135

more children. They were very, very close. My daddy worked on the railroad. I saw how hard my mother worked to keep the family together while my daddy was away. He was always there for my mother. He would come home so tired and my mother would embrace him. In spite of his tiredness, I saw love, and that was what I always wanted."

"I had one sister and no brothers," Lou continues. "My mother kept the family intact by her strength, particularly spiritual strength. She saw to it that we went to school. I always loved school. That's why I love books now. I always had a close affection for my mother. That's where I got most of my strength and most of my desire to achieve or to accomplish something and make something of myself.

"I had to go back to Fort Benning. Then I was transferred to Fort Seal in Oklahoma," Lou recalls. "That was a long way from Atlanta. After two months at Fort Seal they shipped my outfit to Camp Anson. We were on our way overseas. I was stationed in India for the entire thirteen months I was overseas. In January of 1946 I was discharged. When Japan surrendered there was elation all over the place."

"While he was away, I started working as a student librarian," Vivian says. "Being that our daughter was my parents' first grandchild, we had plenty of people to babysit. They wanted me to have the opportunity to do

LOUIS IN THE UNITED STATES ARMY:

DRAFTED 1942;

DISCHARGED JANUARY 1946.

some of the things I wanted to do. I got a chance to go to different places, but basically I worked and prepared for Lou's return. He was interested in black history, so I started gathering information."

"Our baby was eleven months old when I saw her," Lou continues. "I went back to school and encouraged Vivian to go back. She had only a few hours to complete her degree. I finished Morris Brown in '49 and then enrolled at Atlanta University, School of Social Work, to complete my master's."

"When our baby was almost five years old, we moved to Seattle for Lou's first job. We were a long way from home."

"When I finished graduate school, Atlanta University School of Social Work advised me of a job with the Seattle Urban League. They invited me out to take the job with the King County Juvenile Court. I was the first black in any capacity to work in that environment. I was out there three months before Vivian came. It was the first time she had ever been that far away from home without her family being there to give her support. She was homesick. She would cry and I would pet her and tell her, Darling, soon as we're able we're going to move back East so we'll be near home and you can visit. There was no way with my income, just starting out, that I was going to be able to put her on a plane and let her come home every weekend. True to my word, I was able to get a job with the Illinois State Training School for Boys."

"On Saturday mornings we would gather around the table and discuss what had happened the previous week. We would put everything out that hurt our feelings," Vivian explains. "Anything, just bring it out. On Sundays, that was when we had our special time. Our little girl was so cute, if anyone would call on the phone, she would say 'My mama and daddy are in the bedroom taking care of business.' We had our special moments and we made sure that we made time for one another.

"I would say, 'Lou, I don't want to say anything to you; I am angry with you.' Later on, we would make up. Don't get me wrong, we had sunshine and shadows in our marriage and in life, but when you marry, you marry for life. Lou is a good husband, not perfect," Vivian explains. "We are just as different, different as day and night. I am outgoing. I love life and I love people. I love what people have to say and what makes them tick and believe there's some good in everyone, and I try to find that good."

"I am more reserved," Lou chimes in. "My tendency is to be reticent or reserved; it's not because I don't like people. I love people too, but I have a different approach. I usually try to evaluate people on the basis of where they're coming from. I wait and see what their philosophy of life is and if our philosophies can mesh. If our philosophies tend to coincide, then I can be drawn closer to anyone. I deal with our differences that way. I know how she loves to talk and she is a person who makes friends easily. I caution her about that sometimes but give her leeway. I'm not going to try to change her, ever," Lou explains.

"Lou has a hobby that vexes me sometimes," Vivian says. "He loves to clip papers and save papers. It's hard to keep a house going with papers all around. That is one of my pet peeves with Lou, but he knows how to talk me out of it. Lou was in the hospital and I was angry with him about accumulating papers. I wanted to straighten up. I said 'Lord, have mercy, send him back to me so he can clean up these papers.' Little things like that would break up some marriages. We're human."

"I love her dearly and I tell her that all the time. I respect her and have always admired her. Because of that admiration and respect for her I save myself just for her, because I love her very much. I always have and always will. She's the kind of person that has kept our marriage intact these fifty-four years. Even when I first met her I compared her with other girls, and I knew a lot of girls. She was the one that was true blue. I have a friend who had a thing for her and I have enjoyed every moment of it, because I knew he couldn't have her," Lou says.

"The women love him. He's kind and generous to the women," Vivian says. "I can see them eyeballing him. I'm not jealous. I feel like I have Lou; if not, I know that I have tried. I have tried to be a good wife.

"We pray together and personally," Vivian says. "I write inspirational poems; this is how I pray. When I lost my vision, some people would say, why me, Lord? But I think about all the blessings I do have. So many people have not had a husband as long as I have, that stood by me and reads to me. We're not perfect. We have our faults.

"Marriage and love—you have to work at it," Vivian continues. "It's a two-way effort. When you marry you're to be as one, yet you do not lose your identity. Realize that you are both different.

Respect their mood swings. Sometimes, people need to be alone. I don't care how much we love each other, we need some time apart."

"Loyal is one of the things a man should be to his wife," Lou says. "Show emotion to her, tell her that she is loved, not only when she is young and pretty. You don't desert anybody because of age or infirmity. She has lost her sight. I still love her—it's an affliction over which she had no control.

"I consider her a blessing, I really do. When you can go through life with a marriage such as ours, you have to be blessed. I feel very comfortable knowing that she is here for me. Though we have had low points in our marriage, we're together. She's a blessing in more ways that one. I feel good that I have had a life with her. If I were to die tonight or tomorrow I would be completely content, because I have lived with her. She has been my role model as a wife. I don't think I could have done any better. She has had a cheerful outlook on life even during our most depressed moments."

18

May Your Way Be
Smoothed and Brightened

DOROTHY BEARD AND PAUL MCGIRT

Married August 22, 1954 · Franklinton, North Carolina

We met at North Carolina Central University in 1949, which was then North Carolina College," Dorothy begins. "I was a bit withdrawn. I didn't live on campus, so I only saw him when I came on campus."

"She was pretty, soft-spoken, and I saw quality, at least I thought I did."

"He wasn't the type who would force himself on you. He was a little bit reserved, but yet there was something that sort of drew him to me. I'm not sure what it was."

"I looked like a solid citizen. I represented stability, romance, and adventure," Paul chuckles.

"Maybe he fooled me," Dorothy laughs.

"Being a 'war hero,' I had a lot to say. Been some places and seen some things. I guess she was attracted to me for that reason. Also, I was handsome, had money to spend, and was brilliant in my books," Paul smiles. "She came from good stock and in those days you valued good stock and good breeding. With the chemistry activated, we were drawn to each other. We got married two years after she graduated. That was considered a long romance."

"We dilly-dallied for two years," Dorothy replies. "I met his family when they came up for his graduation in 1951. He gave me the ring the year after he graduated."

"A bona fide, expensive, keepsake diamond, $349," Paul recalls. "I'd gone to her house. I met her folks and my impression was that these are good folks, good solid citizens. We had to wait a while because she wasn't entirely sure, nor was her mother. Dot's family is much closer than my family. My folks were a little bit staid and stiff. We all get along together, though."

"My father died when I was a little child," Dorothy adds. "Although I wasn't around my father that long, I could see that he and my mother were very close. In fact, she never wanted to marry again because she was so in love with Daddy, and she didn't. She talked about him the rest of her life."

"In those days we had some appreciation of family ties and relationships between families, how they react to each other and to other folks," says Paul. "When I was a child, growing up in

DOROTHY AND PAUL

ON THEIR WEDDING DAY,

AUGUST 22, 1954, IN FRANKLINTON,

NORTH CAROLINA.

Camden, South Carolina, we had two medical doctors, a dentist, and two drugstores. My daddy had his barbershop on Main Street. We owned a dry-cleaning business. We had basically what the white folks had in terms of businesses. The relationship between the whites and blacks in that town evidently was pretty cordial because I don't recall a single, overt racial incident. Growing up, I was not aware of any. Maybe it was my own lack of awareness. Having attended a Methodist school, Mather Academy, a predominantly black school, and being taught by a predominantly white faculty, I mingled with these folks all the time. That, coupled with the fact that you got all these white-looking folks in the family. My granddaddy was white, grandma was white, and nobody asked questions."

"As we grew up, there were places we couldn't go," Dorothy recalls. "This was the way it was in Franklinton, North Carolina. We didn't have a relationship with whites that we could really see. There were those subtle things like having to go through their back door, go to the back of the drugstore to get an ice cream cone, and they would have to walk all the way from the front to the back to serve you. We were children then and in the early years this didn't affect me like it did later."

"My folks were together fifty-four years, until the good Lord separated them" Paul says. "I never heard a harsh word in the house. As a youngster I noticed this plaque on the wall. This is probably what they lived by. It said, 'As you travel on together over matrimony's miles, may your way be smoothed and brightened by willing hands and smiles. May your sunny

142

days be many, and your cloudy days be few. May you always love each other, whatever else you do.' Mama was always there committed. Daddy was there committed, too. The children were taken care of. I had good examples, good roots. Your upbringing sticks with you. Sometimes you 'escape' it, but most times you don't.

"The fabric of the American family has broken down," Paul explains. "The family now is in shambles, particularly amongst African Americans. It has resulted in a great deal of trauma for all concerned. The root cause of this breakdown is the pursuit of material things."

"As simple as it may seem, setting the table and eating together helps sustain the family structure," Dorothy adds. "Taking time to talk with each other is important. When the family is splintered with the parents going two different ways, the children are gone other ways. They only see each other in passing. The family shatters because there is no togetherness."

"Families are like strangers in the house," Paul points out. "Before you join in a legal union you need to see how compatible you are in terms of your concept of life. It makes a difference. I would investigate that person's background. I would certainly visit the family. How are you accepted into the family? What's your value system?"

"Once you find out as much as you can about one another," Dorothy adds, "and the relationship continues to be strained, I don't think people should be miserable and stay."

THE MCGIRTS STEPPIN'

OUT FOR A NIGHT OF FUN

IN THE SPRING OF 1959.

PAUL'S PARENTS, PAUL SR.

AND JOSEPHINE MCGIRT,

DURING THE LATER YEARS OF

THEIR MARRIAGE.

"Like my old granddaddy used to say," Paul adds, "'If you can't get along together, you can probably get along apart.' If you don't think your love is strong enough to overcome this difficulty between members of your family, then don't do it. Each should go his or her own way. That's cold-blooded but . . .'"

"If the relationship has not cemented during courtship, it's not going to," Dorothy offers. "You can't change a person. The person may conform to some of the things that you want, but the person is not going to change."

"Some alterations and some modifications, but that's it," Paul adds. "I was lucky enough to have good in-laws too, too good to be true. Nothing worse than a situation where you're trapped into it and folks are squabbling, fussing, and fighting. I mean, life is hard enough as it is to maintain your own household. Then you got a mother-in-law expecting she's going to come over and stay two weeks too long."

"In fact, when his mother passed, my school sent a beautiful plant," Dorothy recalls. "I thanked them and made the statement, 'This was my mother-in-law, but she was like a mother.' One of the white librarians said, 'But you said your mother-in-law was like a mother.' She couldn't understand that."

"We've always gotten along, no conflicts, that sort of thing," Paul says. "I'm not particularly close to too many people. More people are close to me, as opposed to my being close to them. I'm a sounding board for all and sundry. I'm a good listener and I can speak if necessary.

144

"Dot is sensitive about keeping the house in order and things being in their proper place. I try to respect that as much as I can, but I do find it difficult sometimes," Paul admits.

"He likes to be on time," Dot replies. "Tell him what time it is and he's going to be there, if not on time then at least an hour ahead of time."

"I'm just too keenly aware of time," Paul explains. "I guess I'm too sensitive, too self-aware to walk in a place late because then I'm the center of attention. I'd rather sneak in the back door if I got to go in late, when everybody's head is turned towards the front. I also like to read and I'm going to read anything and everything. I like supernatural stories, books, and movies."

"Science fiction and all of that Stephen King stuff," Dorothy says.

"I want to sit up all night and watch movies," he says. "I'm going to see *Moby Dick* every time it comes on."

"He watches it every time it comes on, so we watch TV separately because I don't want to watch all that," Dorothy insists.

"We don't see too many movies together because she's got her kind of movie and I've got my kind of movie," Paul admits.

"We've learned to work around our differences," Dorothy smiles.

DOROTHY'S PARENTS, SUPPORA AND WILLIAM (WILLIE) BEARD, AS A YOUNG MARRIED COUPLE.

19
UNDERSTANDING THE POSSIBILITIES

VERA AND THAD TAYLOR

Married December 31, 1965 · Grand Rapids, Michigan

146

After graduating from West Virginia State College, I drove five hundred miles," Vera recalls. "I was out on this open highway following a college friend of mine as far as Detroit. Then I went on to Custer Job Corps in Battle Creek, Michigan, following directions on a piece of paper. I was too young and dumb to even be afraid. When I got there, Thad was working for the same organization."

"I was sitting at my desk," Thad says, "as she walked past the door. I said, 'Gee! Who is that?' I jumped up and ran to the door. 'Who are you, young lady?' She said, 'I'm Miss Smoot.' I said, 'Miss Smoot, what about dinner this evening?' She said, 'I already have a date.' I said, 'I'll accept that, but don't let it happen again.' She went on that date and the next night we went to dinner. From then on we developed a relationship."

"We didn't miss a day seeing each other after work from then until the time we got married," Vera smiles, "except for one weekend when I went to homecoming to see my friends at West Virginia State.

"I saw a mature individual, whom I felt I could trust," Vera continues. "I think there was an attraction, which I might call a soul attraction. Whatever force this was, it made me not go on dates with other guys. We enjoyed each other's company. I think part of that was my desire to know, my thirst for knowledge.

"Thad could talk about so many subjects and I loved to listen to him and he loved to talk," states Vera adamantly. "Can you imagine a young twenty-two-year-old girl having dates with a forty-year-old man and being excited about learning things? Instead of the knight in shining armor sweeping me off my feet, I think everything was kind of old-fashioned. We were happy to sit in the den of the house and talk. I was so far from home and I needed to be careful about people, especially men, whom I might meet in a city, since I came from a small town of about five thousand. This was really a big step for me out in the world. I could trust him."

THE TAYLORS SHARE
A MOMENT WHILE
NEWLYWEDS.

"We were both working for the Job Corps," Thad continues. "It was a program established during the "Great Society" of President Johnson. The program was geared to take the kids who had reached their saturation point in high school, but had not become delinquents. They would go into the training program and come out with skills that they could use to get a job. Even though Vera's office was in our building, her actual work was in another building, so she spent most of her day there."

"When I met Thad," Vera explains, "he took me to meetings about the Baha'i faith. He gave me a book called *Baha'i World Faith*, and I read it. I was astounded by what I was reading. As a child I had lots of questions and few answers. I listened to my elders and I didn't talk back. I just accepted what they said. But once I saw that there was something else, then I knew that they just didn't know. Even though my great-grandfathers were ministers, and my parents sent us to Sunday school all the time, this had nothing to do with my decision. I was on my own spiritual journey. The Baha'i faith just made sense. At first, there was a little period of anger, for not knowing. Then I realized I was from a small town, and this faith was not known everywhere. Before we married, permission from both parents was required."

"Four months after meeting, we married," Thad admits. "After a fifteen-minute ceremony in the home of the man who married us, he drove to Cleveland to his own wedding. Two close friends attended our wedding. It consisted of Baha'i prayers and music.

"It was a simple ceremony that has stood the test of time," Vera adds.

"I had been married before and lived in Denver," Thad continues. "We had two sons. In Denver a man could not file for divorce, so my ex-wife filed. Circumstances regarding my children were beyond my control and led me to leave Denver."

"I should have spoken up more on behalf of the children because when they were ten and twelve they came to visit," Vera says. "We all liked each other and they wanted to stay with us. Everything was set for them to live with us. During the process, they were promised something material if they came back home. When they got back home they called back and said, 'We didn't get anything, Dad.'"

"I knew also that if the kids had come to live with us it would have been constant harassment," Thad explains. "I didn't want Vera involved in that and I didn't want to be involved in it either. I have some regrets about it, but there was nothing I could do under the circumstances. I had to accept that."

"We always wanted children," says Vera, "Thad was a real good father. For instance, I had a hard time waking up at night and he'd always get up and do the feeding because I just couldn't wake up! I was one of those people who needed eight hours of sleep. If I didn't get it, I couldn't manage well. He told me with the second child, I'd manage, and I did!

"Vera seemed to be able to balance the roles of mother and wife. We did mostly family activities including camping, fishing, boating, and bowling. When they went to high school, they no longer wanted to do theses things; however, we continued to have family meals."

"Once the children were older, Thad and I became more involved in the Baha'i faith. I always knew that I wanted to be a mother and raise children. I enjoyed it. I didn't work full-time until my youngest son was six. Before I started working Thad gave me an allowance. He would say, 'This is for you to spend on yourself, not for the house, not for me, and not for the kids.'"

VERA WITH SONS,

DEREK AND ANDREW,

IN 1976.

"I figured she had a right to it," Thad insists. "She's going to take care of the kids, she's not working, she has a right to have some money to spend on herself. I never had an allowance when I was a kid. I didn't even know what the word was."

"He was probably doing what he wished somebody had done for him," Vera chimes in.

"Everything I got I had to work for," Thad continues. "I got a shoeshine box when I was eleven years old and I was out on the corner shining shoes. I felt that she had to have some money for herself, so I put aside some for me and some for her."

"In the beginning we had a joint checking account," Vera says. "But that soon changed. Thad used to travel for his work. During one trip he took the checkbook with him. I had gone bowling with our league and discovered that I had no cash. One of our male friends gave me ten dollars. When Thad returned, I told him what happened. That's when we decided to open separate accounts that each of us had access to."

"We didn't have arguments," Thad recalls. "I think that was one of the contributions I made to this marriage. I decided that we would not argue. We'd discuss things. Sometimes I get loud. It's not arguing. It's not fussing. We just disagree. Once we were chaperones at a dance. When we got home, Vera swore that she smelled someone's perfume on my suit coat."

"There was one woman who was in his face a lot," Vera adds. "I asked, 'Thad, my perfume isn't on anyone else, so how is it that someone's perfume is in your clothes?' Thad could never explain it."

"I still can't explain it today," Thad replies. "At the time, that upset me a lot. Once in a while she'd come back at me with it. I knew I was not guilty of anything. If I had some guilt, it may have been a different story."

"We seldom mention it any more," Vera admits. "I recall Thad pointing his finger at me and saying, 'You'd better not accuse me of anything like that again.' I thought, gosh, he's really serious. He must not be guilty. Let me leave this alone."

"Vera is attractive," Thad smiles. "I had something young and pretty to hang on my arm. One thing about her, she was domestic far beyond most young women."

"Domestic," Vera chimes in.

"I remember, very early in our marriage," Vera continues, "when I was going to shop for groceries and Thad wanted to go. My father never went with my mother, so I thought I was supposed to go by myself. When he wanted to go I said, 'What's the matter, you don't trust me to go by myself?' I was emulating what my mother did. I thought about that later and thought, dummy, you should have let him go with you! He respected that and stayed home. Now, he goes and I stay home! Since Thad's retirement we have reversed roles. He cooks and takes care of the house during the week days."

"I've become the housekeeper and the butler," Thad laughs.

"Thad always made it clear that he wanted a family life. He talked about the value of the mother being at home with the children and the sacrifice that you might have to make. You won't be able to drive fancy cars or take fancy trips, but you forego that for a time to raise the children. Motherhood is a noble profession and now I focus on my career.

"On the other hand," Vera continues, "it takes extra giving on each other's part when you have an age gap, because we're at different parts of the life cycle. Thad's retired and I'm working. I have eight more years before retirement. I feel like I still have something to give to the work world and I want to make a difference. He's already made his difference. He might enjoy retirement better if I were retired, too."

"When you are both active and both working it's no problem," adds Thad, "but when your retirement stage comes and one is retired and the other one is still working, that may create a problem. With the understanding that these are possibilities, you can be more prepared for the disparity in age. Fortunately, we've been able to work through this."

20

Actions Speak Louder than Words

DOROTHY AND CLEVELAND LASSITER

Married December 16, 1945 · Metuchen, New Jersey

We met in the hallway of the administration building at Virginia Union University in Richmond, where they posted schedules and names of individuals who tutored," Cleveland says. "This young lady was standing there and I said, 'Oh, this is my chance to meet her because I need some help with French.' I had heard that she was a buff in foreign languages, especially French. Being the aggressor, I approached the bulletin board and introduced myself. She gave me this cold look. I said, 'I'm Cleveland Lassiter and I need some help in French. Are you available?' She asked me my classification and I told her I was a sophomore. She said, 'If you're a sophomore, I suggest that you get a sophomore to tutor you.'"

"I was a freshman at the time," Dorothy says. "And they told us to watch out for the upperclassmen because they didn't mean the freshmen girls any good."

"That was the first time that I had said anything to her. She gave me the cold shoulder and walked away, but I persisted.

"I was attracted to her; French was a secondary concern," Cleveland continues. "I threw that in as a promotional tool. I had been watching her and could see that she was a very serious student. She worked in the library and I was the cleaning man for the library; therefore, I had to talk to her. It was my job to clean the library after it closed at night and she was preparing books for circulation."

"Cleveland would come to talk with me with this broom in hand, while he was supposed to be working. I couldn't talk to him while I was working." I said, "'Get away from me. You know I don't want to jeopardize my job.'"

"She didn't pay me any attention," Cleveland says.

"I had reasons," Dorothy chimes in. "This nice looking fellow on campus asked me to go out with him. After the date, he came back and spread some terrible rumors about me on campus. I said, 'I'm through with him, I'm through with boys. I'm not going to have my reputation ruined.' I wasn't going to have anything to do with any fellows on campus. The upperclassmen girls had warned me. My friend Rosena said, 'He really wants to meet you,' so we met at the library. I was studying and she

DOROTHY AND CLEVELAND ON THEIR WEDDING DAY, DECEMBER 16, 1945, IN METUCHEN, NEW JERSEY, DOROTHY'S HOMETOWN. THEY MARRIED LESS THAN A MONTH AFTER CLEVELAND RETURNED FROM THE ARMY.

brought him over. They both sat down and she introduced us. She told me, 'Be nice to him, he's a nice fella.' I sort of softened up to boys and gave him a chance. He would call and we would talk and go to the movies. The relationship was gradual. I would still give him a hard time because I needed to fulfill my role as student supervisor."

"We would be back on campus with the other students to see that they got back on time," Cleveland recalls. "She was always rushing."

"Other couples would dawdle back, but I wanted to be on time. I didn't want to have any trouble with the dean of women about not being on campus. They expected more of me because they saw that I had a serious mind."

"Cleveland would take me to church, and I loved going to church. Every Sunday we would go to church, and I loved that about him. We're both from minister's families. My grandfather, who graduated form Howard University, was the pastor of the church where I grew up. Cleveland's father was a minister. We were both children with a religious background. We had certain principles and standards and believe in God, believed in the Bible, and believed in doing what was right.

"It was the longest time before he kissed me. I wanted him to kiss me!" Dorothy exclaims. "I remember the beautiful Christmas tree on campus. It was outside the dormitory and we sang Christmas carols. It was the time of our first kiss."

154

"I picked up right away that she was very shy and played hard to get," recalls Cleveland. "Dorothy was shy but was capable of bringing herself out if she got the right incentive from somebody. I was determined to break that barrier down by showing her the opposite of what I was. I wanted to show her the lighter side of life and other things rather than taking everything so serious. I had to get the message across that age didn't make any difference to me. All the faculty members were about ten to twenty years older than the students. I always made it my job to question everything a faculty member said. She thought that everything that came out of the textbook was Bible truth, and I was just the opposite. I always felt that she was a self-confident person. I was trying to get her to see that I was my own person and age didn't matter to me. I respected older folks but I also thought that they could be misdirected.

"I was getting ready to go into the army," continues Cleveland. "I was going to be leaving campus, so I had to do something to make a commitment."

"He proposed to me in the hall of the library," Dorothy smiles. "We were college sweethearts. One summer I was working in the library and he was stationed at a camp nearby. I reserved a room with his former landlady and got permission from my grandmother to go and live there. The army shipped him the very next week, so the Lord had a hand in keeping us straight!"

"I was scheduled to go in the army on January 30, which was my birthday. I was talked out of going into the army by going into the Army Reserve Corps, which was voluntary. They took me before I finished school. I didn't get my officer's commission because they were so desperate for troops, combat troops in the Engineering Division. If I'd gone in as a draftee maybe I would have gone to Officer's Candidate School, where all my friends became members of the Tuskegee Airmen. I went in saying that I wanted to become part of the paratroopers but they weren't taking any blacks as paratroopers in those days."

"He wrote me practically every day and I wrote him practically every day. Oh! I saved all his letters. I still have them. They were beautiful. He is a most romantic writer," Dorothy muses.

"When he got back, Eleanor Roosevelt warned us not to marry the men right out of the service. She suggested giving them time, so that their personalities would adjust. We didn't pay any

CLEVELAND WITH SONS:
(FROM LEFT) MARK, BRIAN,
AND KEITH IN
THE LATE 1950S.

attention to that," Dorothy laughs. "When I saw him, he said, 'Let's get married.' He returned November 29, 1945, and we were walking down the aisle December 16 of the same year, less than three weeks later. Cleveland wanted the preacher to come and marry us on the spot, but my sister said, 'No, no, no, you have to go home.' We went to Metuchen and had a big wedding. There were over a hundred folks."

"When I came out of the army I went back to Virginia Union to repeat some courses and to finish my degree," Cleveland explains. "We had to live in trailers on campus. GIs were segregated on campus. Dorothy had finished school in '44."

"We were separated for four years. He was in school at Virginia Union and I was working in the government. I would visit him once a month. I was not in Washington the entire time. When we married, I was working for the government and they were closing the agency where I worked. I went to New York looking for a job. I found a job working for the New York Public Library," Dorothy explains. "Cleveland went on to Howard University and got his master's degree in social work.

"Being separated from Dorothy was not an easy job. I wasn't made for that kind of stuff. I wanted to be with my mate. My schoolmates' wives were with them the entire time, but we couldn't work things out that way. Seeing each other periodically didn't quite hit it, but we made it somehow. We didn't let anything deter us with our relationship. After I finished graduate school I moved to New York to join her."

"We were in the Bronx and that was a very unpleasant situation," says Dorothy. "I just prayed and he stayed. I got down on my knees and prayed every night. I prayed my way through."

"Eventually we did get our own place," Cleveland chimes in.

"It was a beautiful brand new apartment in New York, Sedgwick Houses. We were in seventh heaven," says Dorothy. "By then we had our first child. I was so blessed because I worked in the library on the first floor of our fourteen-story apartment building. What better job could you have than to just go downstairs? Soon after, he wanted to move to Pittsburgh, Pennsylvania. Of course my family, who lived in New Jersey, pitched a fit. You would have thought that we were moving to Alaska. I was never a wife to hold him back from what he wanted to do, to dream."

"I was always one to keep moving up or making a change," Cleveland offers. "We went to Soho Community Center in Pittsburgh. It was the second oldest settlement house in the United States. She would go along with whatever decision I would make, not that it was always the wisest, but I was experimental. I wanted to try something new, something different."

"After a year we returned to New York. Cleveland loved his job working for the Lutheran Social Services in New York, but we were having trouble making ends meet," says Dorothy. "We were buying our first home. One day my grandmother came to visit and said, 'This man needs some help. I'm going to stay here and watch these babies until you get a job.' She got the newspaper and she picked the job at Chase Manhattan Bank. She said, 'Go there and go praying.' I went praying and got the job. After working there for a year I missed being in the library field. I went back to get my master's in library science."

"My father always taught us, 'What you are speaks louder than any word that you can say.' He carried himself with respect and he got it from whites and blacks alike. He taught us, 'Don't talk, be. Your actions speak louder than your words. Read widely.' That's the way I was raised," Cleveland explains. "We have had conflicts about raising kids. I feel that you don't superimpose religious choices or preferences on your youngsters. We raised our kids to be pretty much self-determining in making choices about religion or church affiliation. We could have gotten in some serious trouble because Dorothy believes differently. Although we both come from religious backgrounds, my orientation is a little different."

"A lot of difference," Dorothy chimes in. "The man is boss, but a woman has a strong influence on a man. She can make him or break him by the way she carries herself, the way she acts. He wants to hold her up as his wife. He can make or break her too. It works both ways. So many of our young women today, they've lost respect for themselves. We had our minds set on goals. We weren't wrapped up into each other. There were issues bigger than the both of us."

"Women are taking more responsibility and being recognized," Cleveland explains. "Women have been beat back and not recognized for being equal. They have to stand up for themselves."

"It's hard to make a marriage successful," Dorothy admits. "You can't change a person, and Cleveland's tried to change me. He'll say, 'Don't make decisions without telling me.' I'll make decisions and it's hard for me to keep my mouth shut. I was the oldest child in my family and oldest children tend to be bossy. I had to be the mother because my mother died when I was seven. Years into the marriage, I had to sort of pull back, but as I've gotten older that old habit is coming out again. When I would get angry about something, maybe I would cry, but I would not fuss with him because he laid down the rule, 'Don't nag me.' I've never nagged him. He is a different man than other men. You can't compare him. Each person has a different personality that requires understanding. His mother, who passed away at ninety-two years of age, said to me, 'You've done a good job.' She knew that I didn't have an easy time with her son. Before we married they advised me to be very gentle with him. I've always been sympathetic to the black man's struggle."

"I've always had a rebellious attitude against conventional stuff," Cleveland offers. "I can't stand convention. I respect her because of what she believes. She's a very religious person—I respect that. I'm not going to try and change her from that. It hasn't been easy."

"One time one of his jobs did not pay him," recalls Dorothy. "They held a month of his salary, so for two months we had nothing. We had to do something. We delivered telephone books. That was a low point. We had a baby and a child with us and we went to apartment houses deliver-

DOROTHY WITH THE BOYS: (FROM LEFT) MARK, BRIAN, AND KEITH, TAKEN IN THE EARLY 1960S.

ing books in front of each door. We did it together. About handling money, one of my dear friends said, 'I have my money, he has his money, and then we have our money.' That's the way we have done it, too. I handle the checkbook, he handles the savings account. Cleveland gives me the money and I pay most of the bills. I believe that a woman should always have her money. That is what the women always told me. We struggled during the early years. We also helped our families financially. Anybody in my family who had need of money, the money was there, sister or brother. My brother helped us when we bought our house—it was a supportive thing.

"Cleveland has opened a whole world to me that I had never been aware of. I was very rigid and naive, unbelievably ignorant about some things in life. He made me have a softer outlook. There's been a lot of growing up. You get wisdom and you mellow. When you're young you just want to be perfect and you find out you can't be perfect. When you think you're perfect, you have an attitude and then you have a problem. Put God first."

"I don't like to emphasize religion so much," says Cleveland. "Sometimes she gets too close to some of the ministers—I call them jack-legs. She knows more about the Bible than does her minister. People put preachers on a pedestal too much. Life is made up of so many compartments. You have to live a balanced life."

"Cleveland's taught me moderation and I found out that there's a lot of moderation in the Bible that's not preached."

"I think I have the tendency to withdraw or withhold communication at certain times," admits Cleveland. "Sometimes I veil things, but I don't like people to veil things with me. Be forthright, come out with the nitty gritty. I'm reading books now on communication. Every time I find a book on communication in the library I get it. I'm learning, but it's a life-long assignment."

"I can't hold things in," says Dorothy. "It's not good for me, I learned that long ago. I'm a very good communicator, because I say things that I mean, plain and in simple terms. He doesn't say too much verbally, but every holiday, every birthday, he showers me with cards, gifts, and money."

"I would like to be more complimenting to Dorothy, but she knows how I feel," says Cleveland. "I want to make my mate feel that she is the end all, be all. You have to demonstrate with your actions. Make everything on an equal basis. You must seek and search what works for your mate. It's a life-long process of seeking and searching and we have learned from each other."

"I have been happy," Dorothy smiles. "There have been ups and downs, but I have been happy, very happy."

OTHER BOOKS FROM THE PILGRIM PRESS

STRENGTH IN THE STRUGGLE
Leadership Development for Women

BISHOP VASHTI MURPHY MCKENZIE

0-8298-1212-1/136 pages/paper/$12.00

Strength in the Struggle is written for women seeking new direction for their personal and professional growth. It includes a potpourri of information for women, with chapters on such topics as "A Foundation on Leadership," "Defining Moments," "Surviving the Jungle," and "Living beyond Stereotypes." Bishop McKenzie also includes a unique leadership lesson based on the character of Dorothy from the classic L. Frank Baum book, *The Wizard of Oz*.

NOT WITHOUT A STRUGGLE
Leadership Development for African American Women in Ministry

BISHOP VASHTI MURPHY MCKENZIE

0-8298-1076-5/134 pages/paper/$15.95

Bishop McKenzie's best-selling book provides a historical, theological, and biblical overview of female leadership in the church. She suggests a model based on the "Woman Surviving in Ministry" project to promote an environment conducive to learning and dialogue among peers and mentors.

TAKING BACK MY YESTERDAYS
Lessons in Forgiving and Moving Forward with Your Life

LINDA H. HOLLIES

0-8298-1208-3/192 pages/paper/$10.95

"A must read book! Linda Hollies has successfully combined personal honesty and solid biblical storytelling to teach us how to forgive and let go of yesterday.... The prayers will inspire you. The principles will encourage you. The psalms will direct your path." —Iyanla Vanzant, author of *Acts of Faith*.

DAUGHTERS OF DIGNITY
African Women in the Bible and the Virtue of Black Womanhood

LaVerne McCain Gill

0-8298-1373-X/176 pages/paper/$16.95

To reclaim a connection with their deep ethical roots and moral heritage, African American women must learn the stories of strength, courage, and faith. *Daughters of Dignity* seeks to identify these virtues and trace their roots. Gill provides suggestions for self-evaluation and narratives on contemporary programs to successfully reestablish an ethic of black womanhood in the community.

JESUS AND THOSE BODACIOUS WOMEN
Life Lessons from One Sister to Another

Linda H. Hollies

0-8298-1246-6/224 pages/paper/$11.95

Hollies serves up new spins on the stories of biblical women. From Eve to Mary Magdalene, portraits of the bodaciousness of the many matriarchs of the Christian tradition will prove to be blessings for readers. Study questions and suggestions providing examples of how one can grow in faith, of spirituality, and of courage—bodaciousness—are included at the end of each chapter.

MOTHER GOOSE MEETS A WOMAN CALLED WISDOM
A Short Course in the Art of Self-Determination

Linda H. Hollies

0-8298-1348-9/142 pages/cloth/$21.95

Fairy tales will never be the same! Hollies retells classic fairy tales—but with a decidedly spiritual spin. She provides a guidebook for women at the crossroads of their lives while looking at biblical women. The result is a biblical approach to practicing the art of self-determination.

TO ORDER CALL 800-537-3394
FAX 216-736-2206

Or visit our website at www.pilgrimpress.com
Prices do not include shipping and handling.
Prices subject to change without notice.